A MAN'S TURF

A MAN'S TURF

THE PERFECT LAWN

WARREN SCHULTZ PHOTOGRAPHS BY ROGER FOLEY

THREE RIVER PRESS
NEW YORK

Published by Three Rivers Press, 201 East 50th Street, New York,
New York, 10022. Member of the Crown Publishing Group.

Random House, Inc. New York, Toronto, London,
Sydney, Auckland
www.randomhouse.com

THREE RIVERS PRESS is a registered trademark of
Random House, Inc.

Originally published in hardcover by Clarkson Potter Publishers
in 1999.

Printed in China

Design by Elizabeth Van Itallie

Drawings on pages 114–20 and 149 reprinted with permission
from Novartis Crop Protection, Inc., Greensboro, North Carolina.

Library of Congress Cataloging-in-Publication Data
Schultz, Warren.
    A man's turf: the perfect lawn / by Warren Schultz.
    Includes bibliographical references and index.
    1. Lawns. 2. Lawns—United States. I. Title.
SB433.S368   1999
635.9'647'0973—dc21   98-19139

ISBN 0-609-80569-X

10 9 8 7 6 5 4 3 2 1

First Paperback Edition

DEDICATION

For my father, who first turned me loose on the lawn, and for Cathy, who helped me find my way through it.

ACKNOWLEDGMENTS

Thanks to everyone who contributed time and expertise to this book, including: Bill Meyer, Bruce Clarke, and Reed Funk of Rutgers University; Doug Fender of the Turfgrass Producers International; Eugene Roberts of Fairwood Turf Farms; Bill Seccarichia of Winding Brook Sod Farm; landscape architects Doug Reed, Janice Hall, and Pamela Burton; Glenn Smickley, superintendent of the Robert Trent Jones Golf Club in Lake Manassas, Virginia; Dave Berard, superintendent of the Dorset Field Club in Dorset, Vermont; George Hamilton and Shirley Heidrich of Pennsylvania State University; Conrad Johnson of North Carolina State University; Ursula Dean Hoskins of the Central Park Conservancy; Sally McDonough of Mount Vernon; Paula Healy, museum technician, Smithsonian Institution, Horticultural Services Division; Connie Carter and John Sayers of the Library of Congress; Gardener's Supply Company; Bill Borsey of Horticultural Services; Pete Flynn of the New York Mets and Paul Zawatska of the Baltimore Orioles. Also Fay Falcone, Ted Landrum, Alan and Laurie Hilsbury, Tom Mannon, and Gail Gee. Special thanks to Susan Goldberger Newman for encouraging me to write the essay that launched this book; Trixie Vail for her critical eye and constant encouragement; Roger Foley, whose contribution extended well beyond the photographs he shot for this book; Colleen Mohyde, my agent; Elizabeth Van Itallie and Marysarah Quinn for their great design; and Annetta Hanna, my editor at Clarkson Potter, for searching me out to fulfill her vision for this book.

A COMMON THING IS A GRASS BLADE SMALL
CRUSHED BY THE FEET THAT PASS
BUT ALL THE DWARFS AND GIANTS TALL
WORKING TILL DOOMSDAY SHADOWS FALL
CAN'T MAKE A BLADE OF GRASS.

—JUHAN STEARNS CUTLER

CONTENTS

INTRODUCTION

THE LAWN WORKS in mysterious ways. It calls to men with a thick and seductive voice. Though innocent-looking and populated by plants that seem quite unremarkable, that patch of green surrounding our homes commands our attention. It takes our time during the weekend and occupies our thoughts during the week. It pulls us up out of the easy chair and away from the television to tend it. We pamper it, fuss over it, and curse at it. We use it and abuse it. And we expect it to always look its best. We wring our hands when it turns brown or develops bare patches. We puff out our chests when it turns a rich emerald green in the spring. And yes, we mow it every weekend, whether it needs it or not.

Being a man means growing up with a lawn. That's where we learn to ride a bike, on that cushion of green, or learn how to throw a curveball. It's the setting for barbecues and family reunions. It's where we're allowed to spend hours of building daydreams behind a mower.

We trace our lives against those green grids. Our lawns serve as bookmarks for our personal history. We measure our growth by the size and color and condition of the lawn— from the childhood lawn that seemed to stretch to the horizon, to the lawn that surrounded the first house we owned, to the bigger lawn that surrounded our bigger next house.

Of all the influences that make the lawn a metaphor, when it comes right down to it—when the mower blade meets grass blade—our love affair with lawns is a personal thing. For each of us, today's lawn represents all the lawns of our lives. As we step onto the turf, memories rise from it.

◄ Why is this boy smiling? Because he's mowing his way toward manhood, one grassy swath at a time.

The lawn is thick with personal associations. The smell of mown grass and gasoline fumes, like the scent of fresh-baked rolls to Proust, brings powerful memories roaring back. Walking onto the lawn is like stepping through a portal to a safer, less complicated time. That the task of mowing is simple and mindless helps. In a way the job is always the same, whether it's on the front lawn of my youth or the back lawn of my adulthood.

So I crank up the mower. Its roar overwhelms me and blocks out the sounds of the television and the family. The surroundings disappear as I narrow my focus to the green square before me. I start mowing. Immediately the scent of mown grass envelops me.

I could explain away that sharp, sweet smell. I know it's the odor of chlorophyll and carbohydrates created by photosynthesis and released from the clipped blades. In a very real sense, it's the scent of summer sunlight transformed into sweet energy. It's the scent of growth, interrupted by sharp circumstance.

But most of us don't think about where this smell comes from, we just allow it to weave its spell over us. I begin to realize that the lawn is a socially acceptable meditation mat. It's a Zen path through the suburbs.

As I pace the lawn in an ever-tightening spiral, I move farther from the sharp edges of life. The house, the traffic, the people of my life blur and fade into the background. I'm drawn deeper into the lawn with each pass, nearly identical to the previous. I'm working over old ground. I'm lifted out, transported back to other lawns and the aura that rises from them. This lawn is thick with memories of every lawn I've ever cared for. And every lawn is marked with the footsteps of my father. As I work my way across the lawn and get deeper into it, it wouldn't surprise me to see my father striding across the lawn with a mason jar of ice water in his hand, though he's been gone for a dozen years. Gone to that great lawn in the sky. The one where the mower never breaks down or runs out of gas. Where the blades don't clog up with clippings. The lawn without corners where you can just mow forever without turning or backing up.

Here, though, on this earthly lawn, I can picture my dad behind the mower at our old house on a Saturday evening, after all the farm chores are finished. Mowing was not work for him. It was recreation. He'd always change first, from his dusty jeans and denim work shirt, into a flowered short-sleeve shirt and a pair of clean chinos that bore the gray-green stain of grass clippings.

As I mow deeper into the lawn, I can remember the feeling of excitement at the moment when he let me reach up to the handle, put my hand beside his, and walk with him across the lawn. Walk? I'm sure I was practically running, my little legs struggling to keep up with his stride. Though the sharp blades were spinning just inches from my Keds, I felt safe.

◁ And so the young man grows up believing that mowing is best performed while wearing a smile (and perhaps a tie). ▷ Others adopt a more casual mowing attitude and attire; that's my own father taking a new mower out for a spin with me and my brother.

Some days, now, when I'm feeling especially shaky and unsure, I can imagine those father-and-son lawn days. And summoning up the feeling of that firm hand on the handle beside mine keeps me on track.

Some days I can vaguely recall, too, the day my dad decided that I was old enough to handle the mower by myself. No, there wasn't any car-commercial moment with music swelling when he handed over the handles. There were no mowing instructions. Who needs lawn-mowing lessons anyway? You just point it at the grass and go. But it felt like a rite of passage nonetheless. This handover of the mower was typical of our relationship. There were few words involved. There was, instead, example. "Here's the job, go do it, and do it well." It seemed simple then, when I had an example to fol-

▲ Even a small and less-than-perfect lawn spreads out at the feet of its owner, offering a comforting vantage point from which to sit and observe the world. Or just sit…

low. In these complicated days, the lawn helps me relive those simpler times.

I don't think I'm alone. The handoff of the mower handle typifies and symbolizes the way we men are with our fathers, and with our sons. We're often brought together over machinery and a job to do. We don't hand down our businesses anymore. We're not a nation of shopkeepers or farmers. We work for someone else and don't have the ability to lead our sons into the business. They're on their own, and they're just as likely to choose a profession that is nothing like ours. So we hand down our own little backyard business of keeping the lawn trim.

As I mow I still can call up the feelings associated with childhood mowing: pride, excitement, apprehension, freedom. Yes, I felt free, even though my mowing was confined to a green rectangle. Even that confining structure itself was comforting.

So there are days when I'm feeling especially vulnerable that the boundaries of the lawn offer welcome direction. On the lawn I don't have to agonize over direction. I never have to decide which way to turn. Before I know it I find myself back on that country lawn of my childhood.

There were three lawns surrounding our farmhouse when I was a boy. And as each of the sons in the family grew old enough, we took our turns on those lawns. We rotated mowing duty from one to the other.

Each of those lawns was different in nature, configuration, and character. There was the back lawn—

a square-jawed, no-nonsense rectangle. Clotheslines hung over it, with shirts unfurled like flags. There was a water pump in the corner. Paths were worn across it, leading to the cellar door and to the farm fields beyond.

There was the side lawn. Like a parlor in an old house, it was used for entertaining. This lawn was a broad circle, anchored by a weeping willow tree in the center, bordered by hydrangea and spirea bushes and the stump of an old elm tree. This was where the family gathered in the evening to sit on the metal chairs.

There was the long and narrow front lawn. It was a sloping strip that separated the farmhouse from the wetlands and creek beyond. Adults rarely ventured onto this lawn. It was the domain of the children.

In the spring, when the scent and the feel of the new grass called to us kids, we would line up on the front lawn and roll down the hill toward the shrubs. We were answering the need to get close to the grass, to feel it tickling our skin. Throughout the summer and fall, we'd play touch football on that lawn, or we'd engage in sword fights with the long seed pods of the catalpa tree that grew in the corner. Or climb the mountain ash tree at the end and harvest the bright orange berries, string them together to make jewelry for Mom.

I'm sure there were weeds in that lawn, but those aren't the plants I remember. I'm sure it dried up during the summer, got stiff and wiry, but what I remember is the soft cushion of grass that caught and cradled me when I fell. I remember the scent of it on a warm summer evening. Even the taste of it on my teeth.

I remember spending what seemed like entire afternoons staring at a blade, down on its level. I remember the feeling of childhood freedom, the feeling that if I didn't dig my fingers into the grass, I might just fly away.

It was that front lawn, the one that represented pure childish fun, that I chose to mow whenever I had the chance. On a practical level, maybe it was because there was no lawn furniture to move, there were no trees that had to be mowed around. Or maybe it was just an excuse to absorb some of its character of play. For by the time I started mowing, some of that pure childhood exuberance was gone.

The other lawns? Now I recognize what they represented. Call my front lawn the fun lawn. The others, by contrast, were the family lawn and the work lawn. In hindsight I understand my attraction to the front lawn. I recognize the three poles that were pulling at me, and are still pulling at me—fun, family, work—as I bounce from one to the other.

In our lives, as we grow older, the fun lawn shrinks and recedes. We find ourselves spending more and more time trudging through work and family, trying to make time for them, and letting the fun lawn grow shaggy and neglected. We keep trying to get back to that lawn. And any lawn, I think, still holds a hint or promise of those playful sunny summer days.

My care of that front lawn corresponded to my

development into adolescence. In those first years of mowing, I was happy to stay within the lines. The straight-edged structure of the lawn satisfied my prepubescent soul.

Then, one day, as I was entering my teenage years, my father came home with a new rotary mower to replace the old powered reel mower. The blades whizzed around in a blur. Faster and louder, it was like a hot rod compared to an old sedan. It was exactly the right tool for a teenager. It matched my mood.

This new machine epitomized brute strength rather than fussy finesse, and it claimed my teenage heart. With it there was no more getting hung up on tall grass and weeds. There was no more getting stones stuck between the reel blades. And so I realized I no longer had to stay on the established lawn. In time I wasn't satisfied with staying inside the lines. Maybe it was a result of a teen need to challenge the boundaries, but I started expanding the lawn. At the far side, where the row of spirea bushes ended, the lawn was bordered by tall pasture grass and weeds that led down to the wetland. So I started mowing out beyond the border of the lawn, by about half a mower's length each time. The weeds and tall grass fell before the unrelenting, indiscriminating blade of the rotary mower, leaving a wiry stubble that turned brown overnight. But in time it greened up. And began to look, well, lawnish. So I went out a little farther. I kept pushing the edges and expanding my domain. With each

mowing I moved farther out into the wild grass that surrounded the lawn. It was a time of expansion. Hey, it was the '50s. I was responding to an urge to control nature. Perhaps, too, there was some method to my madness. By enlarging the lawn, I was increasing my time behind the mower and so giving myself a few more minutes of solitude and reflection, a few more minutes away from the farm chores and the inevitable progression to adulthood.

The grass was my accomplice. Once I began mowing, the wild grass began behaving like lawn. I was surprised to see my little experiment of imperialism succeed: The grass responded. At first the wild grass turned brown and wiry, but in time it became one with the civilized grass.

It was a symbiotic relationship. I was the instrument that allowed the wild grass to fulfill its destiny. You see, grass can't become lawn without the mower. Just as, in a historical sense, the lawn could not spread without the invention of the lawn mower. Nor could it become what it is today—for better or for worse—without the garden hose, herbicides, and fertilizers.

In my own small way, I was unwittingly acting out the history of the lawn.

➤ The lawn is common ground for men, from the ordinary man to the celebrity, like Humphrey Bogart. When we are on our own turf, we can shed our public personae, the cares of the working world, and our shirts—and enjoy the simple pleasures of our labor.

THE **1** LAWN
GROWS UP

"AND GOD SAID, LET THE EARTH BRING FORTH GRASS....
AND THE EARTH BROUGHT FORTH GRASS..."
–GENESIS 1:11–12

IT'S HARD FOR us to imagine life without the lawn. It seems to cover the country, and it's easy to believe that it always has. But even though grass plants first appeared on earth about 70 million years ago, the lawn is a relatively new idea. It was only within the past 200 years that the lawn, as we know it, was born.

It is true that grasses have been used as design elements in the landscape for thousands of years, dating back, perhaps, to the pleasure gardens of ancient Persia. We know that those walled gardens often included small patches of grass, kept closely cut, but they were a far cry from today's lawns: They were meant to be viewed, not used as today's lawns are. Moving east, around 100 B.C. turf areas were installed in the emperor's garden in China. It took longer for turf to take root in Europe, but medieval gardens of the Continent often included patches of flowery meads. These were plots of turf that were intended for walking and sitting, but they were not made exclusively of grass. They consisted of patches of sod lifted from pastures and included wildflowers and weeds as much as grasses.

◁ One of America's first lawns was planted at Mount Vernon by George Washington.

In the seventeenth century, formal gardens, such as those of Versailles, were designed with large stretches of turf. They were called *tapis vert,* or green carpets, denoting that they were indeed meant to be uniform and, perhaps, trod upon.

In time turf was also put to use in playing fields for lawn bowling, cricket, and golf. The demands of the playing field would eventually turn out to be an enduring influence on the shaping of lawns and on our perception of how lawns should look and behave.

Turf, too, played an important role in the development of the natural landscape style, which was born in England in the early eighteenth century as a reaction against the formal gardens of the previous century. The idea of rolling stretches of turf was championed by many landscapers, including Joseph Addison, who wrote, "If the natural embroidery of the meadows were helped and improved by some small additions of art . . . a man might make a pretty Landscape." Capability Brown, William Kent, and Henry Repton took up the cause, creating landscapes that incorporated vast stretches of turf dotted with trees. However, these parklike gardens were pastoral and pictorial, and the turf was meant for eyes only—to be viewed rather than used.

These areas were not lawns as we know them

▲ In the dark days before the dawn of the lawn, turf grass was utilized as an ornamental plant in medieval gardens, where strips of turf, dotted with wildflowers, served as living carpets.
➤ Naturalistic landscapes of the eighteenth century were manicured and carefully staged approximations of nature; they always incorporated large expanses of turf grazed by sheep and cattle to complete the pastoral scene.

because they lacked an important element: availability. Though perhaps they could be admired by the common man, they could not be duplicated by him. Vast stretches of turf required a great deal of property and labor, as the mechanical lawn mower had not yet been invented, so the grass had to be kept shorn by either grazing sheep or men wielding scythes.

The lawn was a luxury in Europe. It became a necessity and a way of life in America. The lawn was an unfinished idea, waiting for the right circumstances and mind-set before it could flourish. No, the lawn would not really take shape until it reached America. It was here that it found fertile ground; here in the land of opportunity, the land of wide-

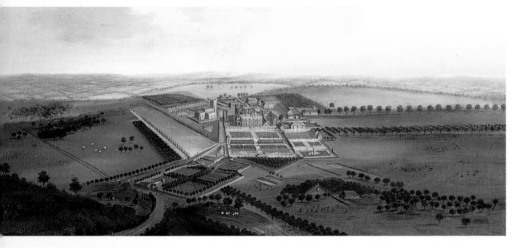

▲ Through most of its history, turf grass has served as a symbol of prosperity. Vast stretches of turf surrounding an estate were signs that the owner was propertied, affluent, and powerful. To this day, the lawn still resonates with that message in large housing developments across the country. ➤ Before the invention of the mower, only those who could afford flocks of sheep or gangs of serfs with scythes were able to keep turf grass mowed in an approximation of a lawn.

open spaces and democracy, the lawn found a home.

When the colonists arrived in the New World, there were no lawns. And there were no lawn grasses. There were meadows and forests. There were native grasses such as broomstraw, wild rye, and marsh grasses. But none of today's turf grasses had yet arrived on the shores of America.

The colonists, of course, weren't much interested in lawns. They had too much real work to do just trying to stay alive. But they did need grass to feed their livestock. And they soon found that the native grasses were not resilient enough to withstand the grazing of the livestock they brought with them. So colonists began importing and planting familiar pasture grasses from Europe—not to prettify their houses. No, their motivation was more utilitarian.

THE SEVEN SPIRITUAL LAWNS OF SUCCESS: A PREAMBLE

Why does the lawn draw us so? Why do we need our lawns so desperately? Yes, we're told that lawns cool the air and cushion the step and filter pollution and cover the ground. But there's more to our love affair with lawns than these practical reasons cooked up by some public-relations bureau in response to the lawn bashing movement of the '70s. The appeal of the lawn is more ancient and visceral than that. The lawn—every lawn, no matter how small, whether in the suburbs or city or country—exhibits a mystical magnetism that cannot be explained in practical terms.

We cling to our patch of turf as though we are holding on to keep from spinning off the earth. If asked why we religiously tend this patch of plants that does not flower or fruit or reward us with any harvest, the best answer is because we have to. For the most part, we are unaware on a conscious level of the charge it sends up through the soles of our sneakers.

(Note: The Lawn Mower Product Safety Commission recommends that one always wear steel-toed boots when mowing the lawn. Right. We're going to spend the money for a special pair of dorky lawn-mowing boots.)

The lawn is lush with meaning. The lawn satisfies needs that we don't even realize we have. The lawn speaks to us if we will only listen, if we will only cast off our twentieth-century sophistication and be willing to endure the jeers of passersby as we bend an ear to the ground.

The lawn is a great suburban mandala laid out before us as a secret path to manhood. It has been given to us as a guide, a secret that has been preserved and handed down through the ages. The farther we get from our primeval roots, the more we need the lawn. It's no coincidence that the lawn has spread over the centuries to meet our emotional need for it.

The lawns that we walk are manifestations of the lawns within us. Everything we need to know about life we can learn while mowing the lawn.

There are seven layers to the lawn, representing the seven spiritual needs of man—oh, all right, woman too, I suppose. I guess the secret is out. We've guarded it for years—the clandestine satisfaction that comes from the mindless task of steering a small engine and sharp blades across a field of green. It was inevitable. With women smoking cigars and wearing suits and getting tattoos and running board meetings, it was only a matter of time before they cracked the grass ceiling and discovered the secret joys of lawn mowing. For years we put on the martyr's face and pretended to grudgingly drag out the mower. "Gee, I'm sorry, honey, I'd love to go shopping with you, but I have to mow the darn lawn." These days you're almost as likely to find a woman behind the mower on a weekend. I guess we have to live with it. As long as we don't have to wash the dishes while they're mowing.

CREEPING ACROSS THE COUNTRY

Perennial ryegrass was one of their first imports. The colonists knew it well. This native of southern Europe and northern Africa had been used as a forage grass in England since the mid-seventeenth century.

They also imported seed of what was then called June grass, *Poa pratensis*. This European native was used in England as a pasture grass, known for its ability to survive hard winters. It almost immediately made a name for itself in America. In fact, it earned its new name in America: Kentucky bluegrass.

June grass found the conditions in America to its liking, and it spread like wildfire. It colonized the territory faster than the colonists did. When Daniel Boone arrived in Kentucky, he found *Poa pratensis* already spreading across the hills. Other grasses soon followed. Many of them arrived accidentally, as stowaways in the ballast of ships. Bermudagrass, for example, an African native, may have arrived on slave ships.

"JAMES TOWNE IS YET THEIR CHIEFE SEAT, MOST OF THE WOOD DESTROYED, LITTLE CORNE THERE PLANTED, BUT ALL CONVERTED INTO PASTURE AND GARDEN; WHEREIN DOTH GROW ALL MANNER OF HERBS AND ROOTS WE HAVE IN ENGLAND IN ABUNDANCE AND A GOOD GRASSE AS CAN BE."
—JOHN SMITH, 1620

The settlers made good use of this new grass. No doubt they evaluated and selected the best examples for their use. But appearance was not a consideration. They didn't care about the color or the width of the blades. All they wanted to know was whether the grass could get the job done—whether it could keep the animals fed. Grasses were measured by their durability and nutritive content. The judges of their virtue were cows and horses.

At that time very few people considered the

▼ Influenced by British landscapes, George Washington planted a great lawn around his Mount Vernon house and became the father of the American lawn.

◄ To this day, sheep still graze on the hillside meadows surrounding Mount Vernon, quietly clipping the turf grass. ➤ But for the public lawns around the house, caretakers have made a concession to convenience, and they use somewhat noisier gasoline-powered mowers to keep the grass trim.

Number of lawn mowers manufactured in the U.S. in 1881: **50,000**

Number of walk-behind mowers currently sold annually in the U.S.: **5 million**

Number of mowers in the U.S. (probably all in operation on Saturday morning—in my neighborhood): **50 million**

ornamental nature of turf grass. Not even the village greens of New England were planted in grass in those days. They were dusty and dirty areas, often strewn with trash and overgrown with weeds. In the villages, houses were built close to the streets. The small front yards were used as garbage dumps. As for the dark and dreary backyards, no one ventured into them.

In time, as the Colonies matured, the European landscape style began to creep into America, along with other trappings of civilization—including lawns. These early lawns of America were experimental and derivative and domains of the rich and powerful. A few forward-thinking men who had time and property began to incorporate lawns into their landscapes. Over time, many of the large plantation houses of the Eastern seaboard were constructed with sweeping lawns that served to complement the house.

It wouldn't be too much of a stretch to claim that George Washington was the father of the American lawn. At Mount Vernon, Washington copied some of the great estate gardens of Europe. He included a

MONTICELLO, THE EAST PORTICO.

▲► Though turfed areas were not totally unknown in Colonial America, Monticello was one of the first residences to be completely surrounded, from the east to the west and all points in between, with a wide swath of lawn.

large circle of turf behind the house and also installed a trim turf grass bowling green on his property.

Thomas Jefferson was also an American lawn pioneer. Swayed by the influence of the great gardens of Europe, such as Versailles, he installed a large lawn dotted with flower beds at Monticello. In his writings you'll find his own critique of Kentucky bluegrass.

THE MOWER MAKES THE LAWN

Yes, there were early lawns in America, but for a century they remained playgrounds of the privileged. The majority of the population wasn't ready for lawns in the eighteenth century. The country couldn't accommodate this symbol of leisure. It would take another century (and more) for all of

the forces to converge to make the lawn.

Though the grass itself spread quickly enough, the idea of the lawn as we know it did not. The lawn could not be fully realized until the time was right. The lawn could not exist until America was ready to embrace the suburban life. It could not blossom until America was ready for conformity. Until then, grass was potential. Grass was like an idea without a voice with which to speak. It was like radio signals without a receiver to convert them. It needed the right set of circumstances to make it practical. Most of all, it needed a lawn mower.

Today the lawn mower is such a cultural icon, it's hard to imagine life without it, but 170 years ago there was no such thing as a lawn mower.

In 1830 the modern lawn mower was invented by Edward Beard Budding in Gloucestershire, England. Employing a series of spinning blades, it was remarkably similar to the reel mowers still manufactured today.

A TIME LINE OF LAWNS

➤ 70,000,000 B.C. The grass family, *Gramineae*, first appears on earth. It adapts to browsing by prehistoric creatures and outlives them, only to be confronted by a more persistent threat: the suburban man, armed with a lawn mower.

➤ 1260 A.D. Turf-covered banks are used as seats in British gardens

➤ 1307 Sod sold for one shilling per 100 turves

➤ 1312 10,000 turves installed on the grounds of Westminster Palace

➤ 1584 First appearance of the word *lawn* in English

➤ 1749 First mention of *Poa pratensis* (Kentucky bluegrass) in North American literature

➤ 1858 Central Park in New York, America's first public park, created

➤ 1871 First lawn sprinkler patented

➤ 1880 47,000 man-powered lawn mowers manufactured in the U.S.

➤ 1900 First motor-driven lawn mower manufactured in the U.S.

➤ 1929 First U.S. patent issued for a power rotary mower

➤ 1965 Astroturf invented; a dark day in the history of grass, as the natural turf in the Houston Astrodome is replaced with synthetic turf

➤ 1973 Royals Stadium opens in Kansas City, its gleaming artificial-turf surface a shrine to falsity

➤ 1992 The United States Lawn Mower Racing Association is founded

➤ 1995 Artificial turf in Royals Stadium is ripped up and replaced with natural turf as the tide turns and grass has the last laugh

➤ 1997 12-year-old Ryan Tripp sets a world record by riding a lawn mower 3,116 miles, from Salt Lake City, Utah, to Washington, D.C. Once there his offer to mow the White House lawn is graciously declined by the National Park Service.

THE BIRTH OF THE MOWER

By all accounts, Edward Beard Budding was a tinkerer. As a thirty-something unemployed engineer and former carpenter, he found part-time work at a local carpet mill in Gloucestershire. It was there, at one of the mills, as he watched the rotary carpet cutters equipped with blades to remove the nap from wool, that the inspiration for the lawn mower struck. One can imagine him standing transfixed in the roar of the machinery as the huge drums rolled, the blades clanking as they passed over carpets of wool.

In a flash of inspiration, he recognized the similarities between carpet and turf and realized that a machine designed to trim one could be altered to create a machine to trim the other. He borrowed the basic concept of a sharp blade rotating on a cylinder, applied it to a portable machine that could be pushed across turf, and the lawn mower was born. Budding formed the Phoenix Foundry with a partner in 1828 to design and manufacture his machine. On August 31, 1830, he was granted a patent on "a new combination and application of machinery for the purpose of cropping or shearing the vegetable surfaces of lawns, grass-plats, and pleasure grounds, constituting a machine which may be used with advantage instead of a scythe for that purpose."

In the patent application Budding noted not only its efficiency but its recreational possibilities. "Country gentlemen may find in using my machine themselves an amusing, useful and healthy exercise," he noted. Almost ever since, mower manufacturers have been trumpeting the fun element of mowing the lawn.

Budding's mower was an immediate sensation. When his early machine was tested at Regent's Park in 1831, the foreman remarked that it did the work of six to eight men with scythes, and did it perfectly.

Other manufacturers jumped into the burgeoning mower market and began improving the machine. Budding's first mower, of course, was hand-powered. A push reel mower, it was remarkably similar in design to the manually powered reel mowers still manufactured today. Others began dreaming up ways to power the machine. In time there were horse-powered mowers, donkey-powered mowers, and (presumably for small lawns) pony-powered mowers. Behemoth steam-powered mowers hit the market, and finally, in the 1930s, gasoline-powered mowers were developed. They all served to make the job of mowing faster, easier, and maybe more pleasurable.

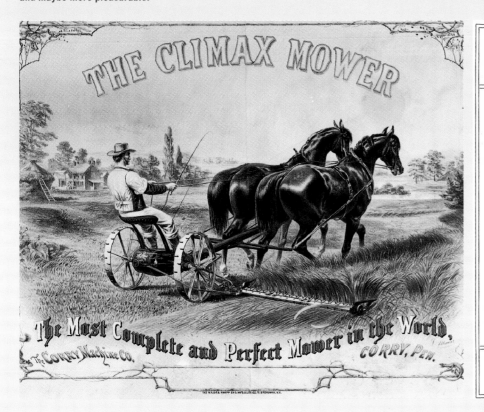

Budding's machine changed the turf in two respects. His inexpensive mowing machine democratized the lawn because it simplified the care of turf for the common man. The gates, in effect, were opened. And the rabble rushed in behind the clanking mower.

Second, the lawn mower was not as selective as sheep, or even men wielding scythes. Nearly every plant fell before its spinning blades. The lawn became more of a monocrop. The lawn mower allowed for more precise grooming. And once that possibility became a probability, it changed our perceptions and our expectations. That theme was to be repeated over and over in the maturation of the lawn. As soon as a refinement—a finer cut, fewer weeds, greener grass—became possible through machinery and chemicals and tools, it became desirable, even necessary. It's ironic that Budding would, in a flash of genius, see that the lawn resembled a carpet. It was because of his vision, and his machine, that the ideal of the lawn *became* a carpet.

It took more than thirty years for the lawn mower to reach America. The first patent for a lawn-mowing machine was issued by the U.S. Patent Office in 1868. Within fifteen years, more than a hundred additional patents for mowing apparatuses had been issued. And lawn mowers became a common item in hardware stores and catalogs. You could probably chart the spread of lawns across America by the growth of the industry.

So the mower was unleashed in America, and found fertile ground. By then, the mood in America was right for the lawn. The country embraced the lawn mower with open arms. England, of course, is a land of walls and fences. But American towns and suburbs were often built in a style that was a conscious reaction against that unfriendly, isolationist fashion. And as the suburbs began to grow in the late nineteenth century, lawns were an integral part of them. The houses were placed on large lots, open to one another. And what better way to fill those lots than grass? Single family homes needed something to surround them, and the lawn mower made it possible to surround them with grass.

➤➤ Apparently pushing a reel mower was not easy enough for everyone, and it didn't take long for inventors to begin tinkering with the mower to find a substitute for muscle power. In the late nineteenth century, mowers were hooked to horses, mules, and ponies for propulsion. ➤ During that time, adventurous investors also strapped mowing decks onto steam engines and continued experimenting until the mower met its perfect mate, the internal combustion engine.

"IT IS UN-CHRISTIAN TO HEDGE FROM OTHERS THE BEAUTIES OF NATURE WHICH IT HAS BEEN OUR GOOD FORTUNE TO CREATE OR SECURE. THE BEAUTY OBTAINED BY THROWING FRONT GROUNDS OPEN TOGETHER, IS OF THAT EXCELLENT QUALITY WHICH ENRICHES ALL WHO TAKE PART IN THE EXCHANGE, AND MAKES NO MAN POORER." —FRANK J. SCOTT, *THE ART OF BEAUTIFYING SUBURBAN HOME GROUNDS,* 1870

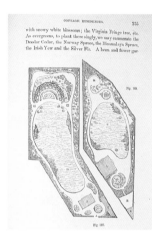

➤ When Thomas Jefferson designed the grounds for the University of Virginia, he incorporated great expanses of closely cropped lawns, grown from seed that he had brought back from Europe. ▲ Eventually the lawn was brought home to the common man by garden writers and landscapers such as Andrew Jackson Downing, whose designs always included lawns as an integral part of the landscape.

The lawn still could not grow, though, without its champions. And it found one in Andrew Jackson Downing, one of America's first landscape architects. He perhaps had more to do with the look of the suburbs—the fenceless, wide-open spaces, lawn flowing into lawn—than anyone. As Downing said, "The close proximity of fences to the house gives the whole place a confined and mean character. A widespread lawn, on the contrary, where no boundaries are conspicuous, conveys an impression of the ample extent and space for enjoyment." Though he is well known for his designs for estates and public parks, including the Capitol grounds and the White House, his real passion was for the home landscape. And virtually all of his landscape designs were dominated by lawns.

Though new homeowners welcomed the lawn, they weren't yet too particular about the grasses that made them. Rough pasture grasses were all that was available, and they were good enough. And no one made a fuss about clover or crabgrass or dandelions. That too would require time to change.

S-6115 G
42 oz
(14 Day)

BUILDING A
BETTER GRASS

THE NEW LAWNS rolling out across America weren't too far removed from pasture or the immigrant grasses that had arrived centuries earlier. They did the job. They covered the land. They cushioned the ground, prevented erosion, and stayed relatively green throughout three seasons. And they framed the new houses without competing with them for attention.

In terms of research and breeding, though, turf grasses fell through the cracks. They were an oddball crop. At first they seemed beyond the purview of the United States Department of Agriculture (USDA), which was busy with agronomic crops such as soybeans, wheat, and corn. In fact, it wasn't until 1912 that the department took its first look at turf grass. And even then it took some prodding and financing from an interested outside party. That party was the United States Golf Association.

With the construction of the first golf course in America in 1888, the game of golf began catching on. As more and more courses were constructed, golf superintendents began petitioning the USDA for help in finding better turf grasses. That increased

◄ Dr. Bruce Clarke inspects a few of the turf plots at the Rutgers University Center for Turfgrass Science, in New Brunswick, New Jersey.

demand led the United States Golf Association to enter into a joint research project at the Arlington Farm in Virginia in 1916.

The USGA provided funds to land-grant colleges to study and breed grass. But their ideal of turf was somewhat specialized and not necessarily what suburban lawns needed. For the USGA, good turf had to meet certain very specific requirements. It had to be low growing and able to withstand close mowing. It had to be relatively weed-free and stay green throughout hot summers and cold winters. Most of the research requested by the USGA involved bentgrasses, the low-growing fussy grasses that are used for golf greens.

The USGA influence went a long way toward shaping the look of the modern American lawn. For the sake of play, certain standards apply: When playing golf, there's a good reason to have a smooth, uniform, short surface devoid of weeds that can mess up a lie. For the purpose of a backyard lawn, however, a

few weeds and long grass don't really matter much.

For decades the game of golf was the driving force behind turf grass research. But in terms of the home lawn, turf breeding lagged behind the continual development of the lawn mower. Though the 1950s (when my father was turning me loose on the lawn) seemed to be the golden age of the lawn, the selection of turf grasses for homeowners was incredibly limited. The few varieties available were rough and unsophisticated. In fact, suburbanites were planting the same grasses in their lawns that ranchers and farmers were using in their pastures. These grasses were green, for sure, but most were stemmy, coarse-bladed, and subject to devastation by insects and disease. They didn't perform well in shade or

poor soil or under extreme weather conditions. Grass, as a crop, was an afterthought. And the thousands of acres of turf that were sown as the suburbs boomed in the '50s and early '60s were inferior stuff.

When "Merion" Kentucky bluegrass was introduced in the 1930s, it doubled the number of bluegrass varieties available in the United States. "Merion" was a breakthrough variety—finer, greener, hardier—that had been discovered growing in an old golf course. Still, it did not result in a flood of new varieties. By 1954 there were still only two Kentucky bluegrass varieties on the market. Then things changed. By 1968 there were thirty-eight Kentucky bluegrass varieties on the market. Today there are more than one hundred. In 1960 there was only one

Turf trial plots are often planted in the worst locations—where soil is wet and the dew lingers long into the morning—to test the grass's ability to stand up to disease and, ultimately, pass the toughest test in golf courses, lawns, and parks.

Dr. Reed Funk, director emeritus of the Rutgers University Center for Turfgrass Science has spent his professional life on the lawn, or at least in the turf grass plots. He's left his mark on lawns across America. Most of the best-known and most highly touted turf grasses released in the late twentieth century were developed under his direction at Rutgers.

perennial ryegrass cultivar available. In 1970 there were seven. By 1997 there were 276.

There's no question there has been a boom in turf breeding, but it's been a quiet explosion, one that most of us have been unaware of.

New technology is partly responsible for this boom, but even today, turf grass breeding is, for the most part, delightfully low tech. The breakthroughs are made not in the laboratory but in the field. The varieties are not so much created as discovered. The preferred technique is not hybridization but selection. And that simply means finding a better grass in the wild, then digging it up, multiplying it, testing it, and releasing it as a new variety or using it as breeding stock for better grass. Even today some of the best varieties are found in the wild.

It's called selection, but what that means is treasure hunting. And it's up to the breeders to get down on their hands and knees and find those varieties that have withstood the test of time. It involves luck, sharp eyes, perseverance, and a strong back. A good grass breeder knows how to keep his eyes on the ground.

A turf breeder's office is the outdoors. He has to believe that the perfect grass is out there underfoot somewhere—in a pasture or a cemetery or public park, on a golf course. He knows that billions of grass plants have spread, and crossed, and endured, and prevailed over hundreds of years. They've been tested by nature—droughts, frosts, grazing animals

GRASS FAMILY TREES

New turf grass varieties are most often bred from germ plasm to existing grasses found in the wild. Here are some Kentucky bluegrass varieties and where their parents were found:

➤ "Mystic" Kentucky bluegrass—at a golf course near Kennedy Airport in New York

➤ "Banner"—on the grounds of Fort McKinley, Maryland

➤ "Midnight"—on the Mall in Washington, D.C.

➤ "Glade"—at the old capitol grounds in Albany, New York. ("It's a good thing I found it when I did," says Reed Funk, "because it's all covered in concrete now.")

—and by man. And the best grasses endure, survive, and spread, perhaps as a small, overlooked patch in the middle of a park or an abandoned golf course. They're out there. It's up to the breeder to find them.

So the breeder travels the countryside, head down, eyes open, looking for a grass plant that's a little greener; has a finer blade; a lower, denser growing habit; or a resistance to diseases and insects— one that is just a little bit better than anything else on the market. When he finds it, he carefully digs it up, takes it back to the research station, plants it, tends it, takes notes. And grows it some more, hoping that maybe within ten years it will make it as a new and improved variety.

THE MANHATTAN PROJECT

Dr. Reed Funk of Rutgers University, New Brunswick, New Jersey, is one of the country's most respected turf breeders. He has spent thousands of

◄ Color, texture, vigor, disease resistance, drought tolerance— these qualities are all recorded for every plot of new turf grass selections and then compared to the results from established cultivars. With 50,000 turf plots, each evaluated twenty times a year, there's a huge amount of data generated to be evaluated by Bill Meyer, the director of the turf grass program at Rutgers, and his colleagues.

hours combing through grass, and his varieties are the stuff of which legends are made.

There was no turf department at Rutgers until 1962. That's when the university asked Funk to found one, even though he had never taken a course in turf science. He was a crops man—corn and alfalfa. Truth be told, he would rather have been offered the sugar breeding job that was open in Hawaii. But he wasn't.

▲ Researchers look beyond and beneath the grass plant itself in search of the perfect lawn. At Rutgers, a soil-mix study is aimed at determining the best soil mix for golf course greens.

Today, he has no regrets. In fact, he notes proudly, "I was the first university scientist in the country hired to do full-time work on turf grass breeding."

Funk got the Rutgers turf program started with a bang. In 1967, within five years of the founding of the turf department at the university, he and his colleagues introduced a revolutionary new perennial ryegrass.

The species was not unknown at the time. It was

used by the truckload to seed the new lawns of the suburbs. For the most part, though, the ryegrass was the variety "Linn," a coarse and stemmy pasture grass. Even so, it germinated quickly and held up fairly well to wear and tear. But because of its shortcomings, ryegrass had earned a bad name as a turf grass.

Then, in the mid-1960s, breeders began to recognize the good points of perennial rye and started

▲ Reed Funk is best known as the father of "Manhattan" perennial ryegrass. Selected from a patch of turf in New York's Central Park, "Manhattan" represented a quantum leap improvement over the only existing cultivar, "Linn." Thirty years later, 90 percent of perennial ryegrass is derived from those original Central Park plants.

to work with it to see if they could coax some of its admirable qualities into the forefront, while eliminating the bad qualities.

Shortly after Funk launched the turf program at Rutgers, he heard rumors of stands of outstanding ryegrasses throughout the Northeast. In particular, word got back to him of patches of outstanding grass in the midst of Central Park in New York City. So

THE FLOWERY MEAD REBORN

Tom Cook is one of the new breed of breeders. He is taking a long, hard look at the lawn, questioning some basic assumptions, and working to return the home lawn to its more natural roots.

Cook's turf trial grounds at Oregon State University in Corvallis look pretty much the same as those at Rutgers. There are the checkerboards of turf grass, some marked with little flags, some with buckets to measure sprinkler performance. There's even a perfectly groomed golf green with cup and flag. But in a small experimental plot over in a corner, Cook is looking beyond turf

grass as a lawn component.

Cook started out searching for the perfect low-maintenance turf grass. His goal was to create a lawn that would require no fertilizer, water only two or three times during the summer, and mowing once every two or four weeks. He soon came to realize that though grass could meet some of those demands, it couldn't meet all of them. He began to entertain a radical notion —that maybe grass isn't meant to grow it alone, that maybe it is at its best when it's grown in mixed company. For Tom Cook realized that grass is not perfect. It takes too

much water in the summer to keep it from going dormant. It requires regular mowing and feeding. So he began to look beyond grass as a lawn ingredient.

Yes, that was a radical idea for a grassman in the 1980s, but not a new idea, by any means. As he researched the history of the lawn, Cook was inspired by the flowery meads of medieval Europe, in which turf grasses were mixed with meadow flowers. So Cook decided to take the lawn back to its roots by introducing other plants into a grass turf. Once he took off those blinders, new horizons opened up to him. "Before, I believed that anything in the lawn that was not grass was a weed," he says. "For years I had been trying to kill broadleaf plants in the lawn. Then I started sowing them there."

He began mixing plant formulas like a mad scientist. Virtually any low-growing, low-maintenance, perennial green plant, whether it was classified as a weed or not, made it into his experiments. He had one overriding requirement: "I wanted a lawn that you could sit on," he says.

In the process he found that there were many, many plants that could do the same job as grass, with less fuss. But many had their own drawbacks. Some of the flowers attracted too many bees. Some were too vigorous and crowded out the grass. Others were too weak and didn't survive. He saw that he

would need to establish an equilibrium, where the flowers would not crowd out the grass or vice versa.

Then he found a breakthrough plant. "Yarrow was the key," he says. "It's incredibly drought-tolerant. It looks good, feels good on your bare feet." In fact, yarrow had been used in golf course greens in the early days of the sport in America.

Ultimately, Cook settled on a mix of 4 pounds of turf grass (preferably Kentucky bluegrass or perennial ryegrass for his climate), combined with 85 grams of other seed—strawberry clover, yarrow, *Bellis perennis*, and chamomile. That's the formula that's now on the market as Ecolawn Ecology Mix. And this idea from the past may help to reshape the lawn of the future.

◄ At Oregon State University, Tom Cook violated the unwritten turf breeder's rule: "If it's not grass, it doesn't belong in the lawn." Turning back the pages to the medieval flowery mead, Cook began mixing other plants with turf grass in an attempt to develop an easy-to-care-for lawn. The result was the low-maintenance Ecolawn, which consists of turf grass, clover, daisies, yarrow, and other plants. It requires less water and mowing than traditional lawns, and it's still soft and attractive enough to enjoy.
► English daisies, *Bellis perennis*, are listed in the weed chapter of most turf managers' handbooks, but they are a welcome part of the Ecolawn turf because of their low-growth habit, drought tolerance, and low fertility requirements. And besides, they look great.

Funk spent a day roaming through Olmsted's landscape, and as he reached the broad stretch of turf in the park known as the Sheep Meadow, he saw it. It was an attention-getting patch of grass: ryegrass, he knew right away, but thick, rich green, fine-bladed.

"The patch was about thirteen feet in diameter," Funk recalls. "It was denser, finer, lower growing, more attractive than not only any other ryegrass in the park, but also any other ryegrass on the market. And since ryegrass reproduces vegetatively rather than by seed, I knew that one seed had produced every plant in that patch. It had spread over the years, so I knew it was persistent. I took a tiller or two out of each plant. And I brought them back to Rutgers."

Then the real test began. Funk and his colleagues planted those tiny plants in plots under several different conditions. They monitored them for a year, and then they picked the best. "So we ended up with a few dozen of the most promising material," he says. They grew them to seed and planted the seed "to see if their characteristics would be transmitted to their progeny." They were. "Then," he explains, "we also had to see if they had a reasonable seed production." They did. "Then we planted them in blocks so each plot would have a chance to randomly cross with sixteen parents."

The result was about 20 pounds of seed of a vastly improved cultivar. But Funk wasn't finished yet. He sent the seed out to different universities to see how this variety would perform around the country and in different climates. When it passed that test, he finally sent the seed out in 5-pound batches to two seed companies. One wasn't interested; the other was. From that 5-pound batch, they planted a 5-acre plot to increase the seed. Finally, in 1967, five years after the plants were discovered, the new variety was ready to hit the market. The only question now was what to name it. It was an easy decision. It entered the market as "Manhattan" and became an immediate success. Lower growing, more wear-tolerant, better-looking, it sold itself.

Since then some 30 million pounds of "Manhattan" seed have been sold. It's been supplanted in the U.S. by its offspring, "Manhattan II" and "Manhattan III," but the original is still being sown on soccer fields across Europe. This variety single-handedly rescued the reputation of perennial rye. Today there are more than a hundred varieties of turf-type perennial rye, and most of them can trace their lineage back to Funk's Central Park find. "Some ninety percent of the ryegrass germ plasm collection today goes back to that Central Park collection," he says.

The Rutgers trial grounds in New Brunswick are still Reed Funk's turf. He strides the checkerboard of 3-by-5-foot plots confidently, wearing a Rutgers baseball cap over his thinning gray hair, with his eyes cast downward. He walks with a slight stoop, the result, no doubt, of decades of bending down to get a

Number of Kentucky bluegrass varieties available in 1960: **6**

Number of Kentucky bluegrass varieties available in 1980: **90**

Number of perennial ryegrass varieties available in 1960: **1**

Number of perennial ryegrass varieties available in 1980: **52**

BREEDERS' TIPS FOR EASIER LAWNS

Scores of breakthrough grasses have been introduced through the turf program at Rutgers, none more important than "Manhattan," which demonstrated to the turf world that a turf grass could combine good looks with durability and still meet low-maintenance requirements. Since its introduction, low maintenance has become a holy grail for breeders. Turf researchers are responding to the needs of the homeowner and searching for grasses that will require less water, less fertilizer, and less frequent mowing. In the process they're casting a new look on old species such as hard fescue.

Here are some keys to growing a low-maintenance lawn:

RELAX YOUR STANDARDS, JUST A BIT

Let go of the idea that a lawn has to be perfectly weed-free and bright green month after month. Adopt the definition offered by Oregon State turf breeder Tom Cook: "A good lawn," he says, "is one that looks good from across the street."

ALLOW THE STRONG TO SURVIVE

If you start with a strong variety and species, well suited to your climate, and if you give it a little bit of care, the strong will survive. Tom Cook calls his ideal the climax lawn. In short, that means that if you start out with a mix of strong grasses adapted to your area, in time the strongest will crowd out the weakest. And the ones that proliferate in the lawn will be the ones that require the least care in the long run.

"Here in the Northwest, for example," he says, "regardless of what you start out with in your lawn, you'll wind up with bentgrass, because it's easy to maintain without a lot of fertilizer."

In fact, Cook has a climax lawn in his own backyard. It's mainly bentgrass with some *Poa trivialis,* some annual bluegrass, and velvet grass.

"Climax lawns are low-maintenance lawns," he says. "If you irrigate them a little, you can even call them turf." When he first moved into his house, he used an herbicide on his lawn to lay waste to weeds. "That's the last time I sprayed, and I can count maybe ten clumps of dandelions there now," he notes.

CHOOSE THE RIGHT SPECIES AND VARIETY FOR YOUR AREA

Though bentgrass, for example, may be low maintenance in the Northwest, it's anything but in the Northeast. There it's known as a finicky, putting-green grass. But there are other grasses that are well adapted and will thrive with little care. There are some new (and not so new) favorites vying for the top spot as a low-maintenance turf: the fine fescues.

"For the Northeast, the best low-maintenance grasses are the fine fescues," says Reed Funk. "There are at least six species of *Festuca,* and there have been many good improvements in all of them." Funk recommends Chewings fescue for New York and New England and throughout the northern tier of the United States. He says that slender creeping red fescue is a good grass for areas with cool summers.

CONSIDER UNCOMMON ALTERNATIVES TO BLUEGRASS

"Sheep fescue, and blue fescue, and hard fescue are all underutilized species that stand out for low maintenance," Funk says. "They're all tolerant of acid soil, low fertility, and moderate shade. On good soils these grasses need very minimal fertilizer. We have turf plots that perform nicely with no fertilizer at all."

Dr. Richard Hurley at Loft's Seed in Bound Brook, New Jersey, agrees. "Hard fescue is certainly underutilized," he says. "But over the past six to eight years it's gained a lot of momentum."

And no wonder. Hard fescue grows very well under cool conditions. It thrives in sun or shade. "Hard fescue is very fine bladed, about as wide as a paintbrush bristle," says Hurley. "Its mature height is about six inches plus a seed head. It's a pretty grass in a nice blue-green color.

"And you can get by with zero fertilizer," he continues. "That's a big, big benefit. It's also slower growing than most other turf grasses, so you can get by with only three or four mowings per year."

THE SPIRITUAL LAWN OF DOMINATION

The first lawn allows us to run roughshod— *(Note: The Lawn Mower Speed and Safety Council warns that one should not operate power equipment at excessive speeds. As though three miles per hour could ever be considered excessive.)* —okay, walk briskly roughshod over small defenseless creatures without a smidgen of guilt.

As adults, as men (and women, I suppose) in the world, we have to tiptoe through our lives. We defer to others. We watch our step. We end up feeling trampled. We're just not allowed to do what we too often want to do: To crush someone under our heels. To chop off their heads. To trample them.

But the lawn offers itself up to us. The lawn allows us to do that. Lawn care is not like the wimpy pastime of flower gardening or the fussy hobby of vegetable gardening. With lawn care, what's involved? You just crank up the mower and go. Straight line. No weeding. No stooping. No, well . . . thinking. The blades of grass fall before you.

The object of lawn care is not to encourage rampant growth and flowering but to control it. Our goal is not to encourage—heck, not to *tolerate*— change, development, and diversity, but to maintain order and sameness. Lawn care is an exercise in control, bordering on domination. Hauling out the mower allows us to obey the male directive to subdue and master nature. Tending the lawn means engaging in a battle—civilized, surburbanized, permissible—but a battle nonetheless.

It's us against the grass.

Those small but irrepressible grass plants struggle valiantly to grow, and if they were permitted to fulfill their destiny, they would flower, and produce seeds, and take over the property. They would return our yards to meadow and wilderness. But we cut them back relentlessly and maintain order.

Tending the lawn is unique among gardening pursuits. It satisfies the need for simple power that's rooted deep in our psyches. Why do you think they call the lawn mower power equipment?

Like nothing else in the modern world, the lawn is unmistakably a man's turf. *(Note: This should in no way be interpreted to imply the abrogation of the rights of women to engage in lawn care.)* It's no accident that the man of the house is the one who's pushing the mower around, while the woman is tending the flower beds, the perennial border, even the vegetable garden. Those gardens are the realm of the women of America. That's because those plantings require nurturing. Those plants must be tended carefully: babied, staked, divided, transplanted. The labor is meant to encourage the plants to grow, mature, and reach their full potential of flower and fruit.

The first lawn allows us to stride forward relentlessly. To let nothing deter us or turn us as we forge ahead, casting clippings and sticks and stones in our wake. For a few hours a week, we may mow mercilessly and feel as though we are in control.

---

closer look at a particular grass plant. It would be easy to picture him puttering over the lawn in a suburban backyard. But his lawn spreads over 60 acres and contains thousands of varieties of turf grass. To a visitor they all look like, well…grass. But Funk is intimately familiar with every one.

"This plot," he says, walking to the middle of a vast field, "shows improvement. You can see some resistance to billbug. And over there you can see some drought stress." Point him to any plot, and he can tell you where the germ plasm came from and when.

!

Years required to breed "Manhattan" perennial ryegrass: **5**

Years required to breed "Rebel" tall fescue: **17**

Funk is still looking for the perfect turf grass. It would be difficult for him to top his early success, but he hasn't spent a moment resting on his laurels. He and his colleagues at Rutgers have introduced scores of new grasses, from ryegrasses to Kentucky bluegrasses to tall fescues.

Like just about every other turf breeder, Funk keeps hoping to strike the jackpot, the perfect Kentucky bluegrass.

For every new variety, thousands of plots have to be evaluated, and observations recorded as many as twenty times a year. "We screen maybe 100,000 Kentucky bluegrass seedlings every year," Funk says. "Out of those we end up with a few hundred that are worth growing out in seed plots, and we're thrilled if we find one of those that's really good. I'd hesitate to say we'll ever find the perfect grass," he says. "But we keep looking. That's job security.

"I've spent many thousands of hours on pastures and old golf courses and so forth," he goes on. "I'm always on the lookout for an improved variety, like an old prospector who keeps an eye out for the sparkle of gold or silver. Ninety-nine percent of the time I come back with a few plants. And once in a while I come back with something that's special."

▼ To the untrained eye, these turf trial plots appear to be a uniform sea of green, but there are hundreds of distinct grass varieties growing side by side, and turf professionals can recognize them all at a glance.

WHERE DID ALL THE CLOVER GO?

It wasn't too long ago that soft, deep-green, low-growing clover was an integral part of a fine turf mix. Turf breeder Reed Funk remembers Kentucky bluegrass and clover lawns from his boyhood in the Midwest. "They were never fertilized and they looked fine. As a legume, a little clover supplied enough nitrogen to make an excellent lawn," he says. "But things have changed. Though clover still crops up in the lawn, today it's considered a weed, and homeowners spend hundreds of thousands of dollars a year in an attempt to eradicate it."

Why? It's a classic example of the homeowners' perceptions being shaped by the turf industry, specifically the herbicide industry.

Clover's downfall began with the O. M. Scott's & Sons Company. The company began as a provider of farm seed in 1870 and eventually became one of the country's foremost turf grass providers. From the early days until the 1950s, clover was included as a component of many of its fine turf mixes. It wasn't considered a weed, and even if it had been, there wasn't much that could have been done about it. In those days, weeds were not a huge concern in the lawn. There was no demand for a perfectly weed-free lawn, because that was not possible; there were virtually no practical turf herbicides. But as the technology of World War II seeped into postwar life, war gases were converted to peacetime use. Scientists soon discovered that by shuffling a few molecules around in the formulas for nerve gases, they could create weed-killers, and the modern herbicide industry was born.

Scott's was one of the first companies to offer lawn herbicides to the public. When they introduced Scott's 4-X, this weed-killer seemed to be a miracle for the way it wiped out broad-leaved plants but left the grass intact. There was only one problem: Clover is a broad-leaved plant. The result? When homeowners applied Scott's 4-X to their lawns, it damaged the clover and left bare spots throughout the turf.

Something had to be done. Rather than giving up on the burgeoning herbicide market, Scott's decided to pull the plug on clover. If you look back through Scott's literature of the late '50s and early '60s, you'll find a gradual but relentless program to discredit clover in the lawn. It starts with articles questioning the value of clover in a lawn and ends with clover classified as a weed, with recommendations for eradicating it. The indoctrination took hold, and today clover is almost universally recognized as a turf weed.

➤ Clover has had its ups and downs over the past century: first an integral part of a fine turf mix; later called a noxious weed; now it's creeping back into fashion.

3 AMAZING GRASS

AS I WRANGLE the power mower across the lawn on a Saturday morning, I can almost hear, above the roar of the engine, a small voice calling out plaintively: "How can you say you love me when you don't even know me?"

No, it's not someone complaining from inside the house. It's not an argument overheard from next door. It's the voice of the lawn itself. And I have to admit, it has a strong basis for complaint.

I know every inch of my property. I know where the buried ledge sticks up through the soil and chips the mower blade if I'm not careful. I know where the backyard stays boggy well into June. I have notes (somewhere) about the shrubs planted along the property line, including variety names and when they were planted and pruned. I study nursery catalogs and memorize tongue-twisting botanic names. I do my homework and know the best plants for the sun and shade and which will survive our frigid winters. But the grass under my feet—that's a different story. It remains a cipher. Even though I spend more time tending to my grass than I do to any other plant, I can only guess at the

◀ At eight to ten individual grass plants per square inch of turf, there are over 8 million growing in an average lawn.

species of the grass in my lawn—or even how many different types there might be there.

But there's one thing that I do know: Each grass plant is a marvel. Any single grass plant in my lawn may be ten, twenty, as much as fifty years old. There may be as many as eight to ten individual grass plants per square inch of turf, or 8 million in an average lawn. And what we see is only a small part of the plant. A little grass plant can produce more than three hundred miles of roots.

And those grass plants work hard. They absorb pollution, catch rainfall, prevent erosion, cushion the ground, muffle noise, and manufacture oxygen. And they just keep growing.

The grass plant is a survivor. We trod on it, roll on it, trample it, neglect it, scalp it—and it comes back. It withstands the winters of Alaska, the droughts of California, the searing heat and humidity of Florida. And it keeps coming back for more.

Grass is a no-nonsense, bottom-line plant. Neither fussy nor temperamental, it gets the job done without calling attention to itself. And that earns our respect. We take comfort in the certainty that the lawn will green up in the spring, and that it will always need mowing. Maybe it's the resilient nature of the grass plant that causes us to admire the lawn so. We modern men can identify with it. We, too, are often clipped just when we think we're growing.

Turf grass is a member of the ancient plant family *Gramineae,* which first appeared on earth during the Mesozoic Period, about 100 million years ago. Over the years more than 7,000 species evolved from this family, including wheat, rice, corn, and bamboo.

The grass plant is also built to photosynthesize. Turf grasses are characterized by short, hollow stems and long leaves. The leaves, or blades, are much longer than their stems. If a maple tree had the same kind of configuration, each of its leaves would be as big as a house. Of course, that means that grasses are photosynthesizing powerhouses. In fact, when it comes to converting carbon dioxide to oxygen, grass plants are four times as efficient in this process as most trees.

LAWN INDEX

➤ Average number of hours spent annually tending American lawns: 40

➤ Total dollars spent annually on lawn-care equipment and products in America: $5.40 million

➤ Acres of lawn in the United States in 1990: 30 million

➤ Number of American households with lawns: 53 million

➤ Annual cost per acre of maintaining a home lawn: $327

➤ Annual cost per acre of maintaining a golf course: $2,000

➤ Pounds of chemicals applied to American turf annually: 70 million

➤ Number of grass plants in a 1,000-square-foot lawn: 850,000

➤ Miles of grass roots under a 1,000-square-foot lawn: 300 million

➤ Number of roots on a single grass plant: 13 million

➤ Miles of roots on a single grass plant: 300

➤ Unleashed and unmown, a single grass plant, such as this tall fescue plant, may grow to more than 1 foot tall and 2 feet in diameter. In the process, it will sport some not-so-attractive seed heads.

It takes 100 growing days for each leaf of a grass plant to become established. The plant itself is fully established when three leaves have emerged.

◄ The grass plant's unique growth habit—ground-hugging crown, creeping stems, and fibrous roots—allows it to spread over hill and dale, forming a thick, uniform carpet.

Of the 46.5 million acres of turf grass in the United States, 23 million acres are in home lawns, 11 million are in commercial sites, 5.6 million are along roadsides, and 1.4 million are in golf courses.

MEET THE GRASSES

Though they all belong to the same family and look pretty much the same to us from behind the mower, turf grass species have many different characteristics, including growth habit, texture, and regional adaptability. Those attributes help to determine which species you should be growing in your lawn.

GROWTH HABIT

Turf grasses are characterized as either sod-forming grasses or bunch grasses. A sod-forming grass, such as Kentucky bluegrass or Bermudagrass, spreads by stolons or rhizomes and knits itself into a strong carpet of sod, leaving little room for weeds to crop up. But a bunch grass, such as perennial ryegrass or blue grama grass, grows in tufts that expand laterally by tillers. This type usually grows faster than a sod-forming grass.

TEXTURE

For most of us, appearance is the most important characteristic of turf grass. And along with color, the most important aspect of appearance is the width of the blade or relative coarseness. It's important enough that all grasses are classified according to their texture—either fine-bladed or coarse-bladed. Fine-textured grasses—such as fine fescues or Kentucky bluegrass—with blades of 6 millimeters or less in width are the most desirable lawn grasses. Coarse-textured grasses, like tall fescue and

centipedegrass, present a less refined appearance in the lawn.

GROWTH REGION

Finally, and most important, grasses are classified according to climate; they are either cool-season or warm-season grasses. Cool-season grasses, as the name implies, grow best in the northern part of the United States. Their prime growth periods there are the late spring and early fall. Cool-season grasses grow best at temperatures between 60°F and 75°F. They may go dormant and turn brown during the hot weather of the summer. Warm-season grasses grow best during the heat of Southern summers at temperatures of 80°F to 95°F.

In turf terms, the U.S. is divided by the so-called Bluegrass Line. Running from the northern borders of North Carolina, Tennessee, Arkansas, Oklahoma, and Texas and through New Mexico, Arizona, and California, this border draws the line between preferred regions for grasses. Cool-season grasses thrive above it, while warm-season grasses predominate south of the line. However, the line is not written in stone. Kentucky bluegrass is often grown in the South and West with regular irrigation, for example. Another cool-season grass, perennial ryegrass, is often sown in the fall in the South to provide color through the winter. And warm-season grasses such as Bermudagrass and zoysia can be found growing as far north as New England.

CREEPING BENTGRASS

TURF-TYPE TALL FESCUE

A CLOSE LOOK AT

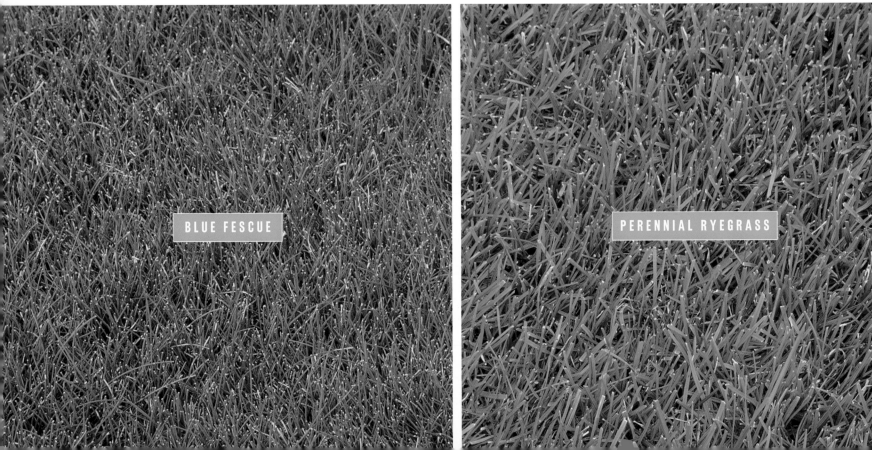

BLUE FESCUE

PERENNIAL RYEGRASS

CHEWINGS FESCUE

CREEPING RED FESCUE

NORTHERN GRASSES

HARD FESCUE

KENTUCKY BLUEGRASS

BUFFALOGRASS

ZOYSIAGRASS

A CLOSE LOOK AT

"TIFWAY" BERMUDAGRASS

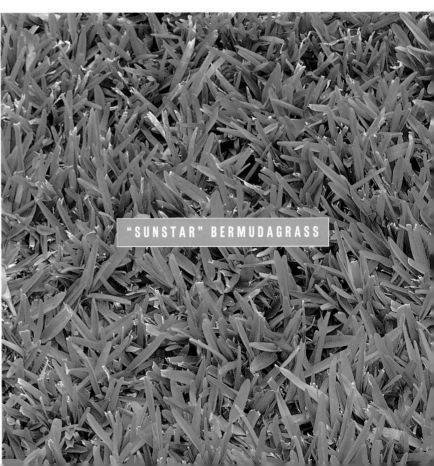

"SUNSTAR" BERMUDAGRASS

"DELMAR" ST. AUGUSTINEGRASS

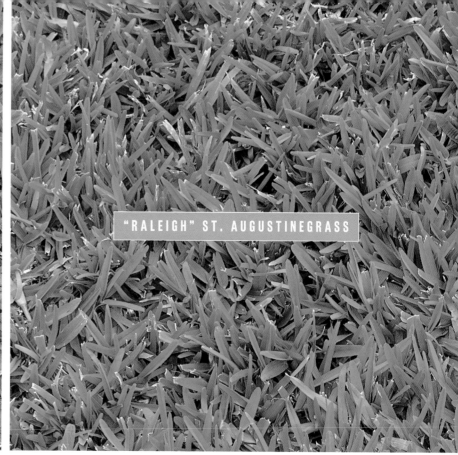

"RALEIGH" ST. AUGUSTINEGRASS

SOUTHERN GRASSES

CENTIPEDEGRASS

BAHIAGRASS

Grass classification offers an important clue to grass care. Cool-season grasses thrive in the cool weather of spring and late summer. That's when they grow fastest. So that's when they need the most frequent mowing and feeding.

Warm-season grasses grow on a different schedule. They like the heat and grow fastest and most vigorously during summer, so that's when they require the most care.

Beyond these major differences among grass types, there are huge variations in how grasses withstand traffic, shade, drought, and other conditions. Like members of any family, grasses have different needs, especially in terms of mowing, feeding, and watering. They vary from species to species and among varieties within those species.

Yes, you can get by without being a grass expert. That's the beauty of the lawn. We don't have to know if we don't want to. But knowing your grass will not only make a better-looking, healthier lawn, it can also mean spending less time and money to maintain it.

Here, in a nutshell, are some of the pluses and minuses of the most common turf grass species.

COOL-SEASON GRASSES

Northern grasses are normally sold in mixes that include two or more species, and perhaps several varieties of those species. This ensures that the lawn will endure many different environmental conditions.

KENTUCKY BLUEGRASS *Poa pratensis*

This fine-textured, sod-forming grass is justifiably touted as the best-looking turf grass. With its thin blades and rich green color, it makes an elegant lawn. But its beauty is more than skin-deep. Kentucky bluegrass is a durable grass, too. It has exceptional cold hardiness as well as good heat tolerance. And most modern bluegrass varieties have good disease resistance. However, Kentucky bluegrass does have some shortcomings. It requires plenty of fertilizer and water to maintain that deep color and is slow to get established from seed. And even with pampering, it doesn't perform well in shade or under moist conditions. Recommended varieties include "Adelphi," "Fylking," "Glade," and "Merion."

CREEPING BENTGRASS *Agrostis palustris*

No grass has a finer texture than this low-growing, sod-forming grass. If you've ever set foot on a putting green north of the Bluegrass Line, you've experienced creeping bentgrass. Soft, thick, and smooth, it forms the kind of carpetlike surface that's required on putting greens, bowling greens, and tennis courts. But it's not made for the lawn. In most parts of the country, creeping bentgrass is extremely demanding. It needs to be kept clipped as low as ¼ inch, and that means mowing at least twice a week. During the summer it requires watering at least as frequently, as well as regular fertilization. However, its relative velvet bentgrass is a good grass for shady areas.

➤ Kentucky bluegrass plants send out creeping stems that root and knit the sod into a thick turf.

Turf grass is a $25 billion per year industry in the United States. It is estimated that more than 500,000 people make their living directly from the care and maintenance of turf in this country.

GRASS PORTFOLIO

Grasses vary in their ability to stand up to environmental conditions. Here's a general guide to the strengths of certain species.

DROUGHT TOLERANCE
➤ NORTH: tall fescue, red fescue, Kentucky bluegrass, perennial ryegrass

➤ SOUTH: Bermudagrass, zoysiagrass, Bahiagrass, St. Augustinegrass

COLD TOLERANCE
➤ NORTH: Kentucky bluegrass, creeping bentgrass, colonial bentgrass, perennial ryegrass

➤ SOUTH: zoysiagrass, Bermudagrass, carpet grass

HEAT TOLERANCE
➤ NORTH: tall fescue, meadow fescue, Kentucky bluegrass, colonial bentgrass

➤ SOUTH: zoysiagrass, Bermudagrass, carpet grass

WEAR TOLERANCE
➤ NORTH: tall fescue, perennial ryegrass, meadow fescue, Kentucky bluegrass

➤ SOUTH: zoysiagrass, Bermudagrass, Bahiagrass

LOW FERTILITY
➤ NORTH: red fescue, tall fescue, meadow fescue, perennial ryegrass

➤ SOUTH: Bahiagrass, carpet grass, centipedegrass

SHADE TOLERANCE
➤ NORTH: tall fescue, hard fescue, Chewings fescue

➤ SOUTH: zoysiagrass, St. Augustinegrass

LOW MAINTENANCE
➤ NORTH: hard fescue, sheep fescue, tall fescue

➤ SOUTH: zoysiagrass

PERENNIAL RYEGRASS *Lolium perenne*

New turf-type varieties of this bunch grass have a much finer texture than that of old coarse-textured cultivars. Since its introduction, perennial ryegrass has become a mainstay in Northern lawns. Rightfully so, since it has many good qualities to recommend it. Perennial ryegrass is a tough grass that stands up well to wear. Improved varieties offer a rich green color without much water or fertilizer. Perennial rye also germinates very quickly and grows rapidly, making it the best choice for a quick lawn. Perennial rye is often sold in a mix with Kentucky bluegrass, where it fills in fast while the Kentucky blue gets established. Several varieties are resistant to insects as well as diseases. Look for "Manhattan II," "Repel," "Citation II," and "Prelude."

RED FESCUE *Festuca rubra*

This very fine textured, sod-forming turf grass is also known as creeping fescue. Shade- and drought-tolerant, it grows well in acidic, poor soil. It's a good choice for the cool, humid regions of the United States. Favored varieties include "Dawson," "Flyer," "Fortress," "Pennlawn," "Ensylvia," and "Ruby."

CHEWINGS FESCUE *Festuca rubra commutata*

This fine-textured bunch grass has a more erect growth habit than creeping fescue. Though it doesn't form sod, Chewings fescue is very aggressive, even in poor, acidic soils. It's often the first choice for a shady lawn. However, it does not stand up well to traffic. Improved varieties include "Agram," "Banner," "Atlanta," "Waldorf," and "Jamestown."

HARD FESCUE *Festuca ovina*

A fine-textured bunch grass, this fescue is often used in low-maintenance lawns. Since it grows slowly, it requires less frequent mowing than other fescues. Like other fine fescues, it has some shade and drought resistance and handles wear and tear reasonably well. "Biljart," "Reliant," and "Waldina" are good varieties.

TALL FESCUE *Festuca arundinacea*

Though classified as coarse-textured, many new "turf-type" varieties of this bunch grass have relatively fine blades and good appearance. This grass is a tough, light-feeding species that's ideal in a low-maintenance lawn. It can grow in light shade and can be allowed to grow as tall as four inches between mowings. Good varieties are "Apache," "Clemfine," "Houndog," and "Rebel."

SOME LIKE IT WARM

There are several species of warm-season grasses, but these types do not include as many improved varieties available from seed. Many of the warm-season grasses must be planted from sprigs or plugs. Unlike cool-season grasses, they are rarely planted as mixed species.

BERMUDAGRASS *Cynodon dactylon*

Fine-textured and sod-forming, this turf grass is tough and vigorous enough to be considered a weed outside the lawn. From Florida to California it makes a turf that thrives on neglect. A good low-maintenance grass, it grows well in poor soils from heavy clay to deep sand, but it turns brown in cool weather. So-called common Bermudagrass, which can be grown from seed, is susceptible to diseases and pests, but new, improved hybrid varieties have good disease resistance. However, they must be started from sprigs rather than seed. Recommended hybrid varieties include "Tifgreen," "Tifway," and "Tifway II."

BAHIAGRASS *Paspalum notatum*

This coarse, low-growing, sod-forming grass grows slowly but eventually forms a thick turf that crowds out weeds. Though good for sandy soil in sun or light shade, the thick-stemmed, dense turf is difficult to cut with a reel mower. Look for the varieties "Paraguay," "Pensacola," and "Tifhi."

BLUE GRAMA GRASS *Bouteloua gracilis*

This fine-textured bunch grass is one of the few North American native turf grasses. As a turf grass, it's especially resilient in the Great Plains states, where it withstands heat, cold, drought, and alkaline soils. Only the species is available, so there are as yet no improved cultivars.

When the temperature of a sidewalk or street is 100°F., the temperature at the surface of a lawn will remain at 75°F.

> "NEXT IN IMPORTANCE TO THE DIVINE PROFUSION OF WATER, LIGHT, AND AIR MAY BE RECKONED THE UNIVERSAL BENEFICENCE OF GRASS. GRASS IS THE FORGIVENESS OF NATURE, HER CONSTANT BENEDICTION."
> —SENATOR JOHN J. ENGALS

BUFFALOGRASS *Buchloe dactyloides*

Another American native, buffalograss is a fine-textured, sod-forming turf grass. It is one of the best grasses for the Great Plains because it tolerates dry conditions and alkaline, clay soils. Buffalograss is a good choice for a low-maintenance lawn in that region because it needs less mowing and less fertilizer than most warm-season grasses. On the minus side, buffalograss turns brown in midsummer and again when growth stops in the fall; seed is also rather expensive. New, improved varieties include "609," "Prairie," and "Texoka."

CENTIPEDEGRASS *Eremochloa ophiuroides*

This coarse grass spreads by creeping stolons. It grows on poor soils, maturing to a height of only 3 to 4 inches so that it requires less mowing than Bermudagrass. However, centipedegrass requires frequent irrigation and turns brown during drought and cold weather. Recommended varieties are "Oaklawn" and "Centennial."

ST. AUGUSTINEGRASS *Stenotaphrum secundatum*

This coarse, sod-forming grass is the best choice for a shady Southern lawn. Under good conditions it forms a thick, dense turf that crowds out all other grasses and weeds. However, it is not a low-maintenance grass as it requires frequent watering and mowing. Favored varieties are "Roselawn," "Better Blue," and "Floratine."

ZOYSIAS *Zoysia species*

Zoysiagrasses are coarse- to fine-textured (depending on the species) Japanese natives that form a dense sod under the right conditions. Often touted as a miracle grass in ads in the Sunday supplements, it's true that zoysia forms a dense, drought-tolerant turf that requires less mowing than other grasses. However, it grows very slowly, taking as long as two to three years to fill in from plug planting. Zoysia has some drought tolerance but must be irrigated in dry areas. Recommended varieties include "Meyer," "Flawn," and "Midwestern."

NEW LAWN OVER EASY

Selecting and buying the proper seed are relatively easy. Turning that seed into a lawn takes a bit of work. Sure, you know that these new varieties are better than the ones in your lawn, but how do you get them there? Even after you figure out which of the new grasses you want in your lawn, the prospect of digging up your yard, no matter how small, seems

Through photosynthesis, 25 square feet of turf will provide the oxygen requirement for one person per day.

ZOYSIAGRASS

KENTUCKY BLUEGRASS

CENTIPEDEGRASS

BUFFALOGRASS

READ BEFORE YOU SEED

New, improved turf grass varieties are slowly making their way into the marketplace. You'll find them in premium seed mixes at garden centers, home centers, and hardware stores. For the most part, you can trust that local stores are selling species and varieties adapted to your region. To be sure, call the county extension agent in your county. He or she should be able to provide you with a list of recommended turf grasses.

While shopping for grass seed, you may have to do a little work to decode the name on the box. While the actual variety names can be found in small print on the back of the box, grass seed mixes and blends are usually sold by a descriptive brand name. The brand name will provide only a clue to what's inside. For example, any name that contains the words *quick, fast, instant,* or *cover* signifies a quick-germinating mix that probably contains a generous amount of the fastest-germinating turf grass: annual ryegrass. But that's something you probably don't want, because annual ryegrass, as its name suggests, lives but a year. The following year your lawn will be left with bare spots, where weeds can invade. However, annual rye's cousin, perennial ryegrass, is nearly as rapid in its germination and establishment. So for a quick lawn, choose a mix that contains a good measure of perennial rye.

The words *family* or *play* on the front of the box offer a good clue that the mix contains a tough, wear-tolerant species such as perennial ryegrass or turf-type tall fescue. Ideally it will contain a modern variety such as "Manhattan II" perennial ryegrass, which is used on athletic fields around the country, or "Mustang" tall fescue, a shade-tolerant variety.

In the North most people want a Kentucky bluegrass lawn for its sheer good looks. The words *estate* or *manor* usually denote the presence of the king of turf grasses: Kentucky bluegrass. Just make sure it's not what is called common Kentucky bluegrass, but one of the new varieties such as "Eclipse."

Once you've gotten a clue as to the content, resist the temptation to be swayed by the bold large type and the gorgeous pictures of perfect lawns. Turn the box over to look at the label. By law every grass seed label is required to list all ingredients, from turf grass varieties to weeds to sticks and stones. First, look for the grasses themselves, listed by percentage in order of amount of content. They will be categorized as to their texture, either fine or coarse. Look for variety names such as "Merion" or "Manhattan" and stay away from those that offer just a generic species name.

Next, take a look at the numbers. The germination percentage of each turf grass is listed. That's simply the percentage of seed that will sprout. It should be at least 75 percent.

Next, you'll find "other ingredients." That may include "weed seed." There will almost certainly be some, but it should be less than 1 percent. The label must also list any noxious weeds, which include those categorized by your state as particularly troublesome, such as quack grass or plantain. There should be none.

"Crop seed" includes grasses that are used as crops such as timothy and rough bluegrass. Though perfectly harmless in the pasture, they're weeds in the lawn.

"Inert matter" includes stones, chaff, and such. There is always some, but it should be less than 3 percent.

CREEPING BENTGRASS

ANNUAL RYEGRASS

THE SPIRITUAL LAWN OF TERRITORIALITY

We've let our guard down. We embrace each other. We bare our souls. We spend our work hours in cubicles and our home days on display in wide-open developments where houses sit cheek to jowl with each other. We need some separation. We need some individualization. We need some boundaries that say "stay out of my face." But America is not a land of fences and hedges. That's why we need the lawn.

As open and inviting as the lawn seems, it's not. It's off-limits. No one would walk across a suburban front lawn unless he or she had a damn good reason for being there. Less threatening and more American than a fence, it's without question a great green moat.

So, as we spend our Saturday afternoons pushing the mower across the lawn, wearing our tattered T-shirts and shorts, waving to neighbors, we're marking our territory. *(Caution: The Lawn Mower Is a Serious Tool and Not a Toy Society cautions that one should always keep both hands on the handlebars when operating lawn mowers and other power equipment.)* The lawn sends a signal to other men. A well-kept lawn is a sign that the man of this house is powerful, in control of nature, and is taking care of business at home.

On the lawn we feel invulnerable, as though we are behind an invisible, impenetrable wall. There we can be public and yet private. The lawn allows us to establish our boundaries.

a bit daunting and makes you think, *Well, this lawn really doesn't look that bad after all.* But it's worth the effort. These new, improved grasses are so much better than the ones on the market just ten years ago, and so much better than the cheap varieties that are usually sown as part of the construction mix for new homes, that it will pay off in no time.

You don't even have to rip up your lawn and start from scratch to start over. The new turf varieties are so vigorous that when the seed is sown over an existing lawn, they'll establish themselves and crowd out the old, weaker grass.

➤ **MOW LOW** To prepare the existing lawn, mow it at half the normal mowing height (as low as ½ inch, depending on the species). Next, with a metal garden rake, rough up the lawn thoroughly, removing all the clippings and as much thatch as possible. Rake vigor-

ously to expose as much soil as possible. Wherever possible, rid the lawn of existing weeds by pulling them up or hoeing them out. If all that hoeing and scratching seems like too big of a job, you can rent a verticutter or slice seeder from a tool shop to do the same job.

➤ **SOW THICKLY** After you've roughed up the sod, it's time to sow the seed. Because you're not working with bare ground, you'll have to sow it thicker. Use 1½ times the amount recommended on the seed package. For example, perennial ryegrass calls for a rate of 4 to 6 pounds per 1,000 square feet; for overseeding use 6 to 9 pounds. Either use a drop spreader or sow the seed by hand, tossing it as you walk slowly over the area.

➤ **RAKE AND TOP-DRESS** After the seed has been sown, rake the entire area with a garden rake.

Then spread a thin layer of sand or topsoil. About ½ cubic yard of soil will cover 1,000 square feet. Finally, water the lawn well, putting down at least an inch of water. Stay off the overseeded area until well after the grass comes up in two to four weeks.

You can, of course, start from scratch and completely renovate your old lawn. But renovating a lawn is a big job. I did it—once. It was, I see now, a symbolic act as much as a practical one. After my father died, my mother talked of selling the house. Maybe it contained too many memories, but for her rationale, she focused on the lawn. It was too big, she said. It was too much for her to tend. If I had still lived nearby, I would have gladly offered to come over every weekend to mow that lawn. It would have been a chance to relive earlier days and walk along with the memory of my dad. But by then I had a home hundreds of miles away. I had my own lawn to tend there. I had my own family to grow and young daughters who would one day take their own turn behind the lawn mower.

So I did the next best thing. Instead of providing continual care for an ailing and infirm lawn, I decided to give my mother a new low-maintenance one.

I dragged the old rotary tiller out from the garage and set it loose on the lawn. This time I had no one's example to follow. I was on my own. And the minute those tiller tines dug into the sod and ripped it apart, I felt a tremendous nostalgia falling over me. It was as though I was uprooting my past.

SEEDING RATES

The size and weight of individual grass seeds vary tremendously from one species to the next. It takes 6.5 million creeping bentgrass seeds to make a pound, for example, compared to 175,000 Bahiagrass seeds per pound. Consequently, the amount of seed needed, in pounds, to seed a lawn varies as well. Here are seeding rates of grass species, in pounds per 1,000 square feet:

Bahiagrass	5
bentgrass	½ to 1
Bermudagrass	1 to 3
blue grama grass	1 to 1½
buffalograss	5 to 7
carpet grass	3 to 4
centipedegrass	¼ to 1
fine fescues	3 to 5
Kentucky bluegrass	1 to 2
perennial ryegrass	4 to 8
tall fescue	5 to 8

And the memories were released as the sod flew—the Wiffle ball games, the pool parties, the backyard wedding. I worked as in a dream until after dark, tearing up the old. I spent the next day raking, digging the old sprigs into a pile and disposing of them. I suppose I could have just left them somewhere to compost, but instead I built a bonfire, more smoke than flame, that smoldered through the night.

By the next day the yard had taken on a new face. It was not the old lawn anymore. It was a bare field full of promise, and I sowed it thickly with seed before I left for home. When I returned, about three weeks later, the new plants had sprouted into a blanket of pale, almost glowing, green. It was the shade of green you don't see on a lawn but once, when it's new. The young grass blades were almost transparent; sunlight seemed to shine through them and cast a green glow on the ground. They were tall enough, and it was time to get out the mower.

THE GREAT LAWN MAKEOVER

The Pope, Paul Simon, and Pocahontas have one thing in common—the havoc their admirers wreaked on the Great Lawn in New York City's Central Park. Granted, the lawn was in tough shape before the appearances of the pontiff, the performer, and the Disney movie, but their more than one million fans trampling the grass were the last straw, prompting Parks Commissioner Henry Stern to declare, "The Great Lawn is a dust bowl." The Central Park Conservancy realized that something had to be done, but its members knew better than to just throw some seed at the problem. So in 1995 they embarked on the biggest and the most closely watched lawn renovation in history. It took two years, more than $18 million, 500,000 square feet of sod, and 25,000 cubic feet of soil to do the job.

Though none of us will ever approach a fix-up like this in our yards, the repair of the Great Lawn offers several lessons for any homeowner faced with the job of repairing an overused lawn.

➤ IMPROVE THE DRAINAGE The Great Lawn was not an original element in Frederick Law Olmsted's design for the park. In fact, the lawn was installed in the 1930s over an obsolete reservoir. Consequently, the 15-acre site acted as a bowl to retain water. To improve the drainage, workers installed three layers of drainage pipe, some as deep as 20 feet in the soil.

➤ IMPROVE THE SOIL The ground beneath the Great Lawn had been packed as hard as concrete by the constant use and abuse by more than 3 million people a year. The soil needed more than repair; it needed complete replacement. After excavating the old soil, they trucked in 25,000 cubic feet of a custom soil consisting of approximately $\frac{2}{3}$ sand, $\frac{1}{4}$ topsoil, and $\frac{1}{10}$ brewery waste. A 20-inch layer of the new soil was spread over the entire area.

➤ GET THE RIGHT GRASS After consulting with turf experts, the Conservancy ordered a special blend of five Kentucky bluegrass varieties mixed with perennial ryegrass. It was grown at a sod farm in Connecticut for one year, and in October of 1996 the sod trucks arrived. A nine-man crew rolled it out at an amazing rate of 50,000 square feet per day.

➤ BE PATIENT Once the sod was down, it was allowed to grow for an entire year before the gates to the lawn were opened.

Now that it's done, you won't see any KEEP OFF THE GRASS signs on the Great Lawn. New Yorkers wouldn't stand for that. And besides, this lawn was built to be used. It's a great urban savanna, meant to lift the spirits of urbanites by connecting them with nature's great emissary: the grass plant.

There will be some rules: no dogs allowed, and at times red flags will appear indicating that the lawn is temporarily closed due to wet conditions. Those rules may drive home the point that, unlike concrete or asphalt, grass has limits to the abuse it can handle. And like New Yorkers themselves, it has its good days and its bad days.

After rebuilding the soil at Central Park's Great Lawn from top to bottom, massive 500-pound rolls of sod were delivered to the site from a farm in Connecticut, where they were grown from seed. The soil was leveled and rolled, and the sod was rolled out. With a single sod roller, the crew of nine was able to lay 50,000 square feet of sod per day.

4 MOW WE MUST

IT'S A CONSTANT refrain: The lawn needs mowing. And we always answer the call. We feed the lawn. It grows. We mow. We water it. It grows. We mow. We ignore the lawn, and it grows, and we mow again. It seems as though the lawn always needs mowing, just as the kids always need a ride to practice or to a friend's house. And we oblige without complaint or question, in much the same spirit for both. We do our duty, because that's who we are; it's part of being a man.

We derive some satisfaction from the knowledge that we are necessary. The children need us. The lawn needs us. Without our regular supervision, both would grow wild and unruly. And we take pride in our ability to perform the task before us. No one else can mow the lawn the way we do. We're the only ones who can do it right.

So we roll out the mower and give the starter a good yank, and off we go. Perhaps we'll pull out the spark plug and give it a cursory examination. We'll change the oil . . . once in a while. We'll sharpen the blade . . . rarely. But we'll mow . . . always.

We might even admit to ourselves that this mowing is more than a chore, that we

◄ Old real mowers were temperamental beasts, likely to jam on the smallest twig or stone.

77

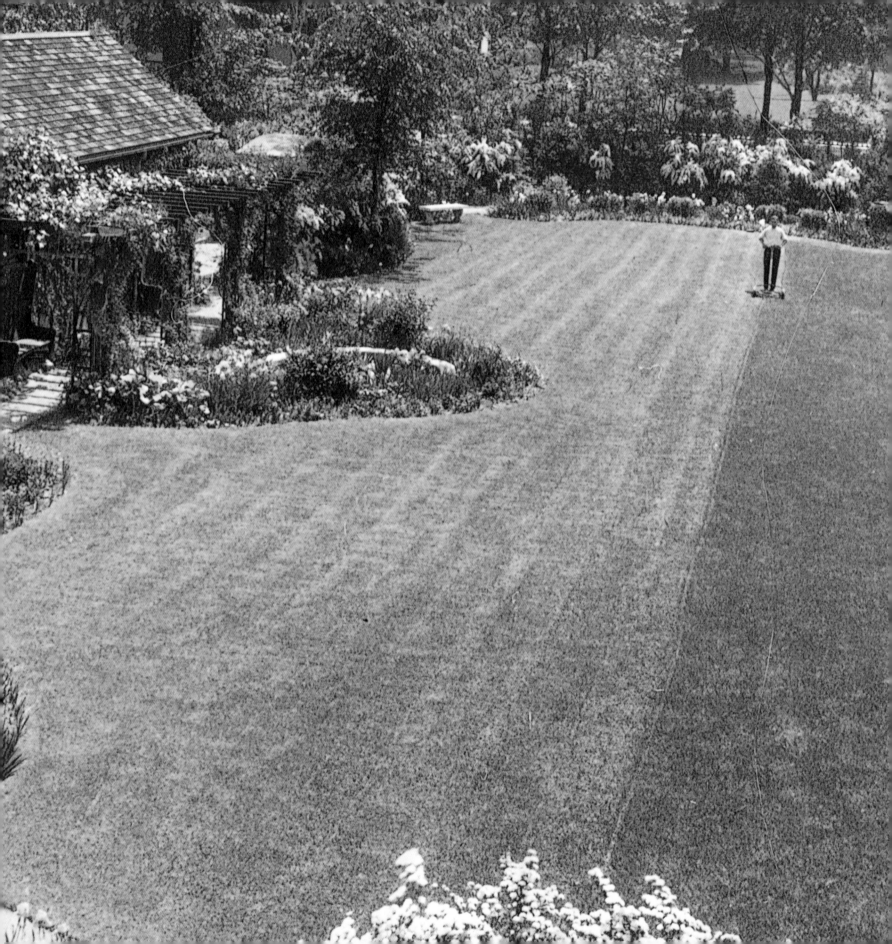

feel at home behind the mower. The act itself seems instinctive. How do we know how to mow? Is it an innate male instinct? No one ever really taught us. There are no mowing manuals. There is no mower's ed class in high school, no learner's permit.

That is part of the appeal of mowing the lawn: We don't have to study and learn and practice. We just mow. Chances are we don't even consider the incongruity of mowing: how such an unnatural act could feel so natural to us. Mowing is unique among garden chores. Normally we feed and water and tend the plants in the garden in order to get something—flowers, fruit, or vegetables. But in this case, the harvest—a heap of inedible, unattractive, virtually useless clippings—is worth less than the act of harvesting itself.

If we think of those leaves of grass at all—sliced and diced and sent flying, hundreds of them every second—we must admire the resiliency of the lawn and marvel at how it manages to take this abuse every week without skipping a beat. After all, it takes some of us days just to recover from a haircut.

It's no secret: Turf grass was made to be mowed. It's in its genes. For grass evolved under millions of years of grazing pressure. As food for animals, the plants that survived were the ones that withstood constant browsing. Their defense was to develop a specialized growing habit with the growth point hugging the ground at the crown of the plant. The turf grass plant doesn't present its tender new

HOW TO BUY A MOWER

Eventually your old mower is going to go to the great lawn in the sky. Unfortunately, when it comes time to shop for a new one, we're usually at a loss. As soon as we walk into the shop, we're seduced by the biggest, shiniest, fastest, most powerful mower on the floor. That's what we all want, but maybe that's not what we all need. Here's a checklist for making a wise choice at mower-buying time:

CHOOSE A REEL MOWER IF

➤ Your lawn measures less than 2,000 square feet

➤ Your lawn is composed of grasses that can withstand mowing at two inches or below

➤ Your lawn does not contain tall, tough weeds such as plantain

➤ You've got time to kill

➤ You need exercise

CHOOSE A PUSH OR SELF-POWERED ROTARY MOWER IF

➤ Your lawn measures up to one acre

➤ Your lawn contains coarse-textured grass or weeds

➤ You're not averse to the roaring of a small engine at work

➤ When shopping, look for
  – Mulching blades: These specially configured blades, usually two blades mounted at a ninety-degree angle to one another, will chop clippings into fine pieces and blow them downward, eliminating the need to bag clippings
  – Cutting height adjustable from 1 to 4 inches
  – Horsepower of 5 to 6.5
  – Smooth and rust-resistant deck
  – Cutting width of 20 to 22 inches

CHOOSE A BATTERY-POWERED MOWER IF

➤ Your lawn measures less than 5,000 square feet

➤ You're concerned about noise and exhaust pollution

CHOOSE A LAWN TRACTOR IF

➤ Your lawn measures one acre or more

➤ You mow at least weekly

➤ You would rather ride than walk

➤ When shopping, look for:
  – Mulching blades
  – Cutting height adjustable from 1 to 4 inches
  – Horsepower of 12 to 18
  – Hydrostatic rather than belt drive

growth at its tip, but produces it at the base, where it's well protected. As it matures, it pushes the older growth upward toward the sun, toward the browsing sheep or the running mower, offering it up and so staying forever young. Its plant memory, the very essence of what it is, is kept closely held.

With our mowers we play the role of the browsing animal. Call it steer envy—that fresh grass smells so delicious and compelling, we just want to eat it. We can't, so we do the

◄ Yesterday's mowers with their exposed wing nuts, hoses, and glass air filters gave men plenty to fiddle with as part of the mowing ritual. ► The 1950s Henderson Contour Mower was built low and wide to provide a short golf-course-green-type cut at home.

next best thing and graze it mechanically with our lawn mowers.

MOWING IS GOOD

Turf grass has developed a response to mowing or grazing. The plants are irrepressible spreaders. They'll reproduce sexually—by setting seeds—if given the chance. But if their cycle is interrupted, if the plants are clipped before flowers can form, the plants' backup survival method kicks in. They

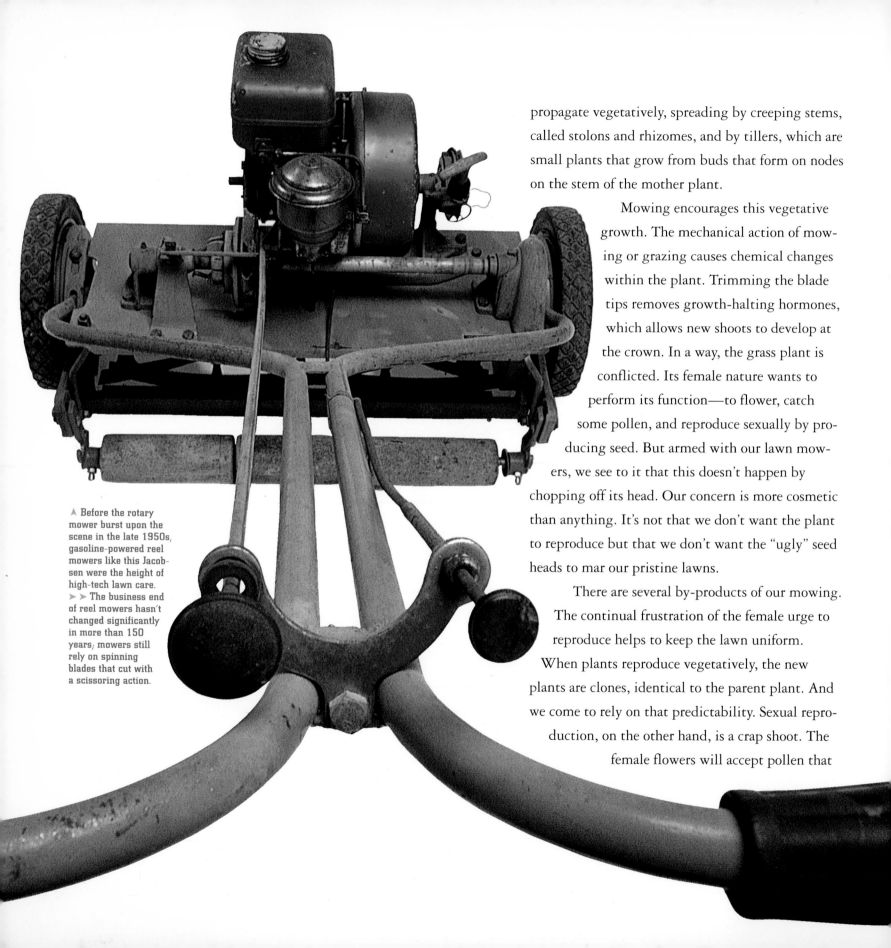

propagate vegetatively, spreading by creeping stems, called stolons and rhizomes, and by tillers, which are small plants that grow from buds that form on nodes on the stem of the mother plant.

Mowing encourages this vegetative growth. The mechanical action of mowing or grazing causes chemical changes within the plant. Trimming the blade tips removes growth-halting hormones, which allows new shoots to develop at the crown. In a way, the grass plant is conflicted. Its female nature wants to perform its function—to flower, catch some pollen, and reproduce sexually by producing seed. But armed with our lawn mowers, we see to it that this doesn't happen by chopping off its head. Our concern is more cosmetic than anything. It's not that we don't want the plant to reproduce but that we don't want the "ugly" seed heads to mar our pristine lawns.

There are several by-products of our mowing. The continual frustration of the female urge to reproduce helps to keep the lawn uniform. When plants reproduce vegetatively, the new plants are clones, identical to the parent plant. And we come to rely on that predictability. Sexual reproduction, on the other hand, is a crap shoot. The female flowers will accept pollen that

▲ Before the rotary mower burst upon the scene in the late 1950s, gasoline-powered reel mowers like this Jacobsen were the height of high-tech lawn care.
➤ ➤ The business end of reel mowers hasn't changed significantly in more than 150 years; mowers still rely on spinning blades that cut with a scissoring action.

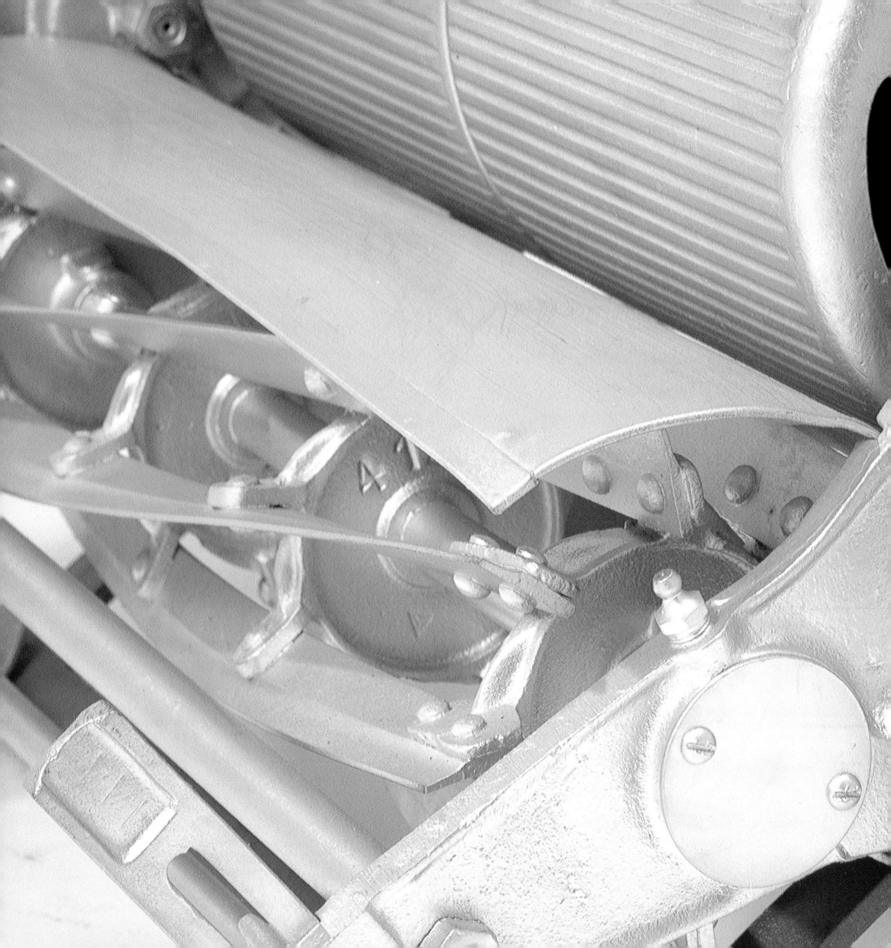

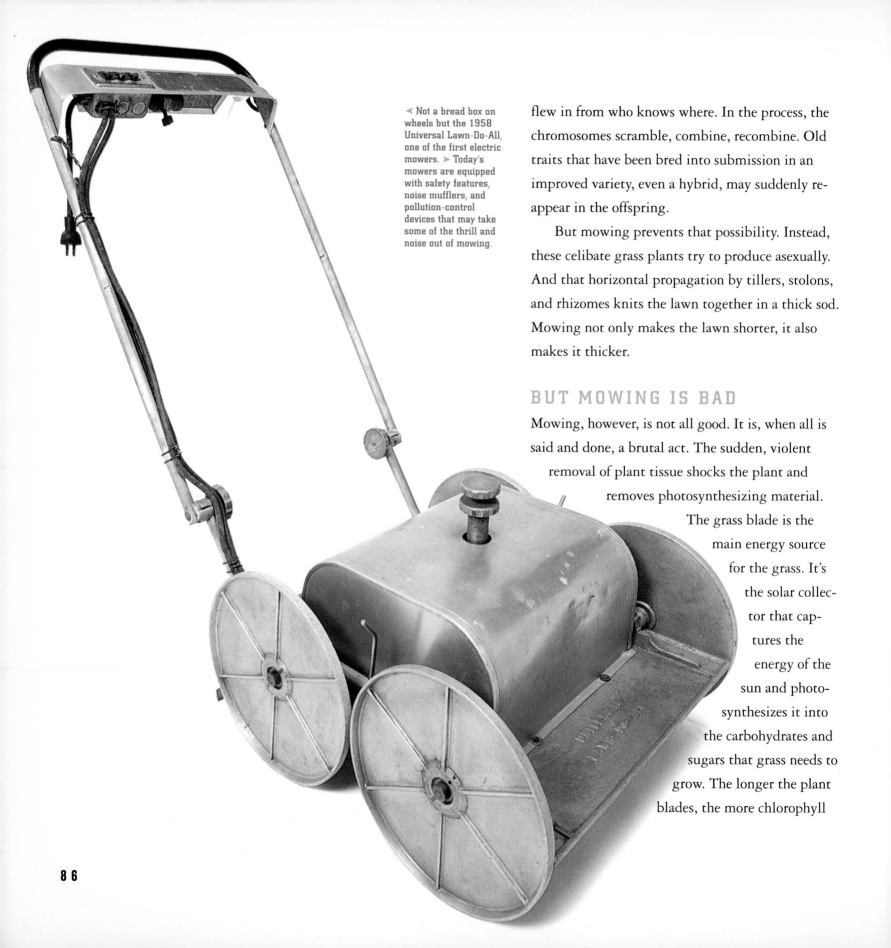

◀ Not a bread box on wheels but the 1958 Universal Lawn-Do-All, one of the first electric mowers. ▶ Today's mowers are equipped with safety features, noise mufflers, and pollution-control devices that may take some of the thrill and noise out of mowing.

flew in from who knows where. In the process, the chromosomes scramble, combine, recombine. Old traits that have been bred into submission in an improved variety, even a hybrid, may suddenly reappear in the offspring.

But mowing prevents that possibility. Instead, these celibate grass plants try to produce asexually. And that horizontal propagation by tillers, stolons, and rhizomes knits the lawn together in a thick sod. Mowing not only makes the lawn shorter, it also makes it thicker.

BUT MOWING IS BAD

Mowing, however, is not all good. It is, when all is said and done, a brutal act. The sudden, violent removal of plant tissue shocks the plant and removes photosynthesizing material. The grass blade is the main energy source for the grass. It's the solar collector that captures the energy of the sun and photosynthesizes it into the carbohydrates and sugars that grass needs to grow. The longer the plant blades, the more chlorophyll manufactured, the stronger and greener the grass. When we mow the grass, we reduce its surface area. The closer we cut, the less energy produced by the grass. Root length is also directly proportional to blade length. Tall grass makes long roots. The longer the roots, the better the plant is able to scrounge for moisture and nutrients.

THE HAPPY MOWING MEDIUM

It's up to us to steer the mower down that fine line between help and harm. Mow too infrequently or too high, and the turf thins out and weeds and disease crop in. Mow too often or too close, and the plants lose vigor. At the same time we must strike a balance between good horticulture and good neighborliness. Mow too short, the grass struggles. Mow too long, the neighbors call the turf police.

Unfortunately, it's impossible to name one ideal height for all grasses. Though they all look pretty much the same to us, grass species have significantly different growth habits. Some grow best when they're closely cropped, others when they're allowed to get a bit shaggy. And it gets more complicated, because the ideal heights vary from season to season. During times of peak growth—spring and fall in the North, summer in the South—grass can withstand a shorter mowing. However, when it's stressed—by summer heat in the North or winter cold in the South—the grass should be allowed to grow longer.

REEL VS. ROTARY

To mow with precision, your mower must have an adjustable bed, allowing for cutting heights from 1 to 3 inches. One of the advantages offered by today's rotary mower over the old-fashioned reel mower is versatility. Reel mowers are at their best when cutting close, where they provide the kindest cut for the grass, snipping the grass like scissors rather than tearing it. Reel mowers are precision machines. That's why they're still used on golf greens, where grass may be kept cut as short as $1/4$ inch. But they

MOWING SCHOOL

There are a few simple rules that can make mowing easier on the grass:

➤ MOW LIGHTLY AND FREQUENTLY

Whatever the season, and whatever the grass, you should mow lightly, following the sacrosanct rule of one third—never cut off more than one third of the grass blade at any one time. Hacking off more than that stresses the grass too much. For example, for a Kentucky bluegrass lawn in spring, the correct height is 2 inches. So you should never let it grow past 3 inches, or else you'll be removing more than one third of the blade when you cut it back down to 2 inches.

➤ ADJUST YOUR SCHEDULE

In the summer it might take the grass a week to grow an inch. In the spring, though, it may grow that much in three days. You should mow according to the grasses' growth schedule rather than the calendar on the wall. When the lawn is growing fast, mow frequently, every time its height has increased by one third. When it slows down—during summer in the North and winter in the South—don't cut unless it needs it.

➤ ADJUST YOUR CUT

Increase your mowing height by one quarter to one third during stress (grass stress, not personal stress) to allow the plants to retain more surface area. Mow higher in shady spots for the same reason.

➤ VARY YOUR ROUTE

With each pass of the mower, you should overlap your previous path by about one third of the width of the mower. This will ensure a uniform cut across the lawn. However, you should alter your path occasionally, perhaps monthly. Running the mower in the exact same route week after week creates ruts in the lawn and compacts the soil under the wheel tracks.

➤ SHARPEN THE BLADE REGULARLY

When mower blades are dull, they smash and pummel the grass blades rather than cutting them. The resulting ragged ends take on a grayish cast and make the lawn look shabby. They also make the grass more disease-prone. Under normal usage, a mower blade should be sharpened monthly.

➤ A vast sea of turf grass flows uninterrupted across the suburbs of America. Each resident is charged with the responsibility of keeping his lawn in conformity with the others.

have trouble cutting grass that's taller than 2 inches —a height that many turf grasses prefer.

Still, for more than one hundred years the reel mower ruled. It was such a remarkable invention, and so far advanced from the scythe, that for more than a century the design remained virtually unchanged.

Even though lawn mowing, right from the start, was portrayed as a relaxing, enjoyable endeavor, that was a questionable claim with the cranky, heavy, muscle-powered reel mowers that many of us remem- ber from childhood. They required constant adjust- ment; they jammed on tall grass and weeds. And they were just too darned quiet. Reel mowers didn't satisfy our need for speed and power and noise.

Throughout the life of the reel mower, inventors tinkered with the basic design: adding grass catch- ers, altering the number of blades, and experiment- ing with power sources—steam, horses, electricity, and finally, the internal combustion engine. When mounted on a reel mower, the gasoline-powered engine provided the speed we needed, but it also nearly sounded the death knell for the reel mower by opening the door for an entirely new design of mower—the rotary.

The brute power of the gas engine allowed the creation of a machine with an entirely different method of cut. Rather than using a number of blades turning at a relatively slow speed on a verti- cal axis, the rotary employed a single blade, mounted horizontally and spinning at dizzying speed—up to 130 miles per hour. Instead of scissor- ing, it sliced and diced. And the mower deck was designed to take advantage of the turbulence cre- ated by the spinning blade to create a suction to hold the grass upright for a uniform cut. In 1933 a patent was issued to William Beazley of St. Peters- burg, Florida, for this new rotary mower, and lawn mowing would never be the same.

Just as the gasoline engine, when harnessed to the automobile, led to the expansion of the suburbs,

HOW LOW SHOULD YOU MOW?

Grass should be mowed at the low end of the optimum mowing height during spring and fall, and allowed to grow a bit longer during summer.

Best Mowing Height in Inches		
	Spring and Fall	Summer
Cool-season Grasses		
creeping bentgrass	¾	1¼
Kentucky bluegrass	2	3
fine fescue	2	2½
tall fescue	2½	4
annual ryegrass	2	2½
perennial ryegrass	1½	2½
Warm-season Grasses		
Bahiagrass	2	3
Bermudagrass	½	1
buffalograss	2	3
carpet grass	1	2
centipedegrass	1	2
St. Augustinegrass	2	3
zoysiagrass	½	1

THE SPIRITUAL LAWN OF BELONGING

Like all powerful symbols, the lawn is layered with meanings, and they often seem contradictory. For while our front lawns separate us from other men, they also join us together in a powerful cabal.

We are bound together, yet operate privately, in our grassy obsession. Pick any moment on a summer Saturday morning, and millions of men are walking virtually the same line, lulled by the same roar, seduced by the same scent. *(Note: The Lawn Mower Muffler Association recommends that you always wear ear protection when operating power equipment to protect whatever hearing you may have left after standing in front of the speakers at heavy metal concerts.)* We follow almost identical paths across virtually interchangeable lawns in a virtual million man mow.

So while it is a tool of privacy, the lawn is a sign of neighborliness and conformity. The lawn is like a businessman's dark suit; the flower borders represent a loud tie, chosen by his wife. A well-kept lawn shows that we are abiding by the rules of society and the neighborhood. It signals others that we conform to the unspoken rules of neighborhood design. (Sometimes these rules are not so subtle. In certain communities, homeowners are required to keep 75 percent of their lots in turf grass. In other communities, homeowners must keep the lawn mowed at a height under 3 inches.) Why? Anything else is subversive, un-American. There might be communists hiding in the weeds.

So the Second Spiritual Lawn allows us to satisfy our deep need to belong. Through the lawn we can join others without having to deal with the unpleasantness of actually talking to them.

---

it also, when hooked to a mower, allowed us to expand our lawns. Mowing became easier, so lawns could be larger, and those booming suburban developments could be carpeted with turf from one end to the other.

Loud and fast, and usually bright red, these new mowers were more like toys than tools. They satisfied a need in American men of the 1950s. And once someone thought of putting a seat and steering wheel on them, we were off and running. There was no keeping us off the lawn.

Even today we remain caught up in the speed and the power. We buy bigger and faster machines. We race to get the lawn mowed as quickly as possible. As much as we like being out there, once that engine starts roaring we're hell-bent to finish the job —and end the guilty pleasure it provides. Every week we're in a race against our neighbors. We peer over across the hedge to gauge their progress. We open the throttle to full speed. And we smirk when we get our lawn done first.

OFF TO THE LAWN MOWER RACES

"I've always enjoyed cutting the lawn," says Mike Boris of Harmon's Woods, Maryland. "But like everybody else, I always dreamed of making the mower go faster." Fantasizing about faster mowers didn't satisfy Mike, and fortunately, as the service manager of one of the largest John Deere dealerships in the state, he had the means and the know-how to do something about it.

"In 1990 I bought a used riding mower," he explains. "But it just didn't go fast enough for me. So I souped it up." By the time he had finished monkeying with it, he had more than doubled its speed. It soon became a common sight (and sound) to see (and hear) Mike racing from lawn to lawn in the neighborhood.

Two years later he discovered that he wasn't alone in his quest for mower power. He found some kindred spirits when he attended a United States Lawn Mower Racing Association (USLMRA) race in nearby Havre de Grace. One look at those middle-aged men racing their brightly painted mowers around a short oval track at up to 50 miles per hour —careening around the corners and racing for the checkered flag—and he was hooked.

These days Mike has a racing team of six drivers, including his wife, Mary Lou, and son, Josh Knapp, with a garage of eight customized mowers sporting names such as *Mow Lady* and *Taz Mower.* He'll load up the mowers and drive up to sixteen hours to get to a USLMRA race.

The USLMRA was formed in 1992 as a promotion by the Sta-Bil fuel stabilizer company after one of its employees attended a lawn mower race in Great Britain. Now the association sanctions more than a dozen races a year, from Seattle, Washington, to Presque Isle, Maine. Participants are awarded points ranging from five for first place to one for, as the rule book states, "just showing up." Racers may

➤ Roaring around a dirt track at speeds up to 60 miles per hour, lawn mower racers from Herkimer to Havre de Grace put their man-hood on the line and raise the fun of mowing to a new level. There's noise, there's speed, there's the smell of a four-cycle engine, and, most important of all, there's competition.

enter any one of four classes, from factory experimental to "slow-mow," which Mike Boris calls "the Harry Homeowner class." Anyone can enter a backyard mower in this class. No modifications are allowed; racers just remove the blades, pump a little extra air into the tires, and start their engines. In fact, Mary Lou Boris races with the same mower that Mike uses to cut the lawn at home. Its top speed is about 4 miles per hour. Some of Mike's custom racing mowers move more than ten times as fast, though. Their speedup is accomplished by changing the size of the engine pulleys and modifying the governor that restricts the engine speed on normal mowers.

But the machine that all mower racers dream of, the famous *Dixie Chopper,* has had some more serious modifications. It's equipped with a 150-horsepower Chinook helicopter engine. With that jet engine, it can reach a speed of nearly 70 miles per hour and can mow an entire football field in fourteen minutes.

Though Mike's mowers may never reach that velocity, he spends most of his free time trying to tweak a little more speed out of them. He keeps them tuned up in his backyard garage and on a test track just down the street. One evening while he was putting one of his mowers through its paces on the street in front of his house, he roared past a car that was doing about 30 mph. It wasn't until he flew by that he realized he had just passed a police car. He held his breath, waiting for the sound of a

FROM THE MOW ZONE TO THE OZONE

Though the push reel mower nearly disappeared from commerce in the 1970s, it has recently made a comeback. Why? Not so much because it cuts well, but because it cuts cleanly—environmentally speaking. Few of us give it a thought when we're mowing, but the power mower is a gas guzzler and a significant source of air pollution. The 90 million gasoline-powered garden tools—including mowers, trimmers, tillers, and leaf blowers—send more than 6 million tons of pollutants—such as hydrocarbons, carbon monoxide, and nitrous oxides—into the air every year. In fact, running a lawn mower for one hour releases as much hydrocarbon as driving a car for eleven and a half hours.

The U.S. Environmental Protection Agency, however, is subjecting mower manufacturers to increasingly more stringent regulations aimed at reducing pollution by making the mower engines cleaner-burning. In fact, the next mower you own may be equipped with a catalytic converter.

Say you don't care to push a mower around the lawn? Maybe you think you've come too far in your life for that. One company has an ingenious alternative: the Dynamow. It's a reel mower assembly that attaches to the back of a mountain bike, so you can pedal your way to a mown lawn. Or if you'd rather go the high-tech route, the Poulan Weedeater Company manufactures a limited number of a Jetsonesque solar robot mower. You can watch one clip your lawn from the hammock for only $2,000.

> Over the years, every conceivable means of propulsion has been enlisted to make mowing even easier and more enjoyable, and now as mower manufacturers are compelled to comply with new regulations aimed at curbing polluting fumes, along comes the Dynamow, the world's first pedal-mowered mower.

siren that never came. He figures the policeman just couldn't believe his eyes.

Wherever he goes with his mowers, Mike attracts a crowd of the curious and disbelieving. After people finish laughing, he says, they all want to know how they can get involved in lawn mower racing. He directs them to USLMRA headquarters in Glenview, Illinois. Participation is booming, says USLMRA president Bruce Kaufman, with more than three hundred members nationwide. Or, as he puts it, "We're gaining mow-mentum every day."

The official mower racing season kicks off every year with a Grass Cutter's Ball held, appropriately enough, on April Fools' Day.

Popular mechanics from the 1950s. Gee-whiz, Mr. Science utopianism comes to the lawn as an inventor demonstrates his robot mower from the comfort of a hammock in New York's Central Park.

HOW TO STRETCH YOUR PRECIOUS MOWING TIME

What's the rush? What are we going to do once the lawn is done? Watch TV? Go shopping? Clean the bathroom? Why not stretch out this precious, private time behind the mower? We've got plenty of other jobs with deadlines. Why turn lawn mowing into another one of them? Why not revel in the time behind the mower and allow yourself to succumb to the rhythm of the grass?

How? Short of trading in your mower for a scythe, there are several ways to prolong your mowing time.

USE THE SMALLEST MOWER POSSIBLE

It's simple geometry, or algebra, or something like that: Consider the lawn a two-dimensional area, and your lawn mower the tool for dissecting it, or dividing it into strips. The smaller the divisor, the more strips. The more strips, the longer it takes to divide it.

When it comes to the size of the blade, every inch counts. Suppose you have an acre of lawn to mow. If you were to mow it with a 24-inch-wide blade, you'd walk 4.9 miles to mow the entire lawn. With an average mowing speed of 3 miles per hour, you'd be done in about an hour and a half. Then what? That would leave you with plenty of time to clean the lint out of the dryer, I suppose. But downsize to an 18-inch-wide machine, and you'll have to make many more passes to cover the lawn, and travel nearly 7 miles in the process. Estimated mowing

time with an 18-inch mower? Two hours and eighteen minutes. That gives you another forty-five minutes to yourself—three quarters of an hour to escape the realities of real life. (There is one exception to this rule: The ride-don't-walk postulate states that in terms of psychological satisfaction, fifteen minutes astride a riding mower equals an hour behind a push mower.)

MAKE SURE THERE ARE PLENTY OF OBSTACLES ON THE LAWN

That estimated mowing time assumes that you have a clear field of mowing. But if your lawn is littered with obstacles—trees, shrubs, flower beds, swing sets, dog houses, discarded garden tools and hoses, old tires, sticks and stones —it will slow your trip tremendously. You'll spend time mowing around them, moving them, backing up, moving forward. You can easily double your mowing time with several well-placed hazards. Resist the pressure to decrease your mowing time by mulching around trees, shrubs, and garden beds.

DESIGN THE LAWN WITH PLENTY OF CORNERS AND RIGHT ANGLES

Forget about the circle being the classic shape: for a lawn, it's the rectangle, and right angles and edges significantly increase your time tending it. Think about all the time you waste getting in and out of those cor-

ners. You're cruising along the straightaway when you hit a corner. You stop, back up, maneuver the mower in and out of that cul-de-sac. You eventually get back on the straight and narrow, but before you know it, you roar right up against the next corner. And there is always a next corner. Even after you make a complete circuit of the outside edge of the lawn, the corners are still there on the next pass of the lawn. They move inward with you until the end, when the lawn is nothing but corners. In fact, as you mow toward the center of the lawn, the straightaways get shorter, so the corners get proportionately larger. These lawn corners symbolize life's greater problems: The more you just let them be, the bigger they get.

Of course, some obsessive smart aleck, type-A personalities will tell you that you can eliminate those corners. When you get to the first corner, they say, cut across it in an arc, leaving the point of the corner unmown. Do this at all four corners, and for all intents and purposes, the corners have been expunged. On the next circuit around the lawn, you can travel in one long, uninterrupted ellipse. And when you've finally finished and have mowed to the center, then, and only then, return to the unmown corners and quickly dispatch them. That way you deal with each corner only once. That's much more efficient, they say. But aren't we efficient enough in the rest of our lives? Shouldn't

our lawns allow us the opportunity to do things the hard way?

MOW WHEN THE GRASS IS WET

The clippings will clump up and clog the underside of the deck and the discharge chute. That means you'll have to keep stopping to clear away the green gunk. That could easily double your mowing time. Sure, it's bad for the grass, but who are we out here to please, the lawn or us?

DON'T MOW UNTIL THE GRASS EXCEEDS ITS MAXIMUM HEIGHT

See above.

BAG THE CLIPPINGS

You'll have to stop every few minutes to empty the bag. And because you're depriving the lawn of fertilizer by removing and discarding those nutrient-rich clippings, you'll get to spend even more time on the lawn, spreading fertilizer later.

USE AN OLD MOWER

An old mower will keep breaking down. And time spent fiddling with a carburetor or jiggling a spark plug wire is almost as satisfying as time spent mowing.

FERTILIZE LIKE CRAZY

Along with stretching out the amount of time for each mowing, you can increase the frequency of mowing with some overenthusiastic fertilizing. The more you feed, the faster it grows, the more you mow.

5 THE THIRSTY LAWN

"HE SHALL COME DOWN LIKE RAIN UPON THE MOWN GRASS: AS SHOWERS THAT WATER THE EARTH."
—PSALMS 72:6

WATERING THE LAWN may rival mowing for sheer satisfaction. There's something about a summer evening that makes us want to stand in the middle of the front lawn with a hose in hand. As the water flows and the scent of barbecue smoke hangs, we're at peace. And though we may wave to the neighbors driving by, this sprinkling is a solitary pursuit. Just us and the lawn. The family is inside, watching TV or washing the dishes, and we're right where we belong.

We succumb to the swishing sound of water under pressure and feel the pulse of that water rushing through the hose. And on those very hot summer evenings, a scent rises as the cool water hits the hot dirt. It's an earthy smell unlike anything else. And perhaps the stream of water catches the beam of fading sun and sends up rainbows in the mist.

Earth, air, sun, water—all the elemental powers converge on our little patch of lawn. And with a hose in our hand, we seem to be at the very center of them. Stress flows out of us like water streaming out of the hose.

The grass is at rest. After a long summer day of conserving water, its stomata open.

◄ In order to thrive, a 1,000-square-foot lawn requires more than 600 gallons of water per week.

The Standard Rain King

or the average lawn or garden. Sprinkles revolving or stationary. Throws any spray stream. Each nozzle a sprinkler in itself. Bearings of bronze and *free from pressure*. Sprinkles efficiently on low or high water pressure. Sturdily constructed and the most efficient sprinkler made.

Price $3.50; Denver and West $3.75

The Majestic Rain King

Stands taller than the Standard Rain King to throw water over tops of nearby plants. Bird bath base attracts feathered songsters. Gives all sprinkling actions of the Standard Rain King. Oversize bronze bearings, *free from pressure*, are used in Rain Kings exclusively.

Majestic A
15 Inches High—Price $6.50
Denver and West $7.00

Majestic B
24 Inches High—Price $7.50
Denver and West $8.00

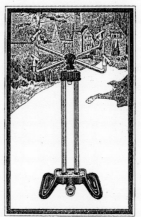

The Majestic C Rain King

Has double brass water columns, 24 inches high. Each of the four all-brass nozzles fully adjustable to any Rain King setting. Bird bath base a very attractive feature. Because of *free from pressure* bearings will sprinkle on any water pressure from 7½ lbs. and up. The Majestic C will sprinkle 5500 square feet at a single setting on 45 lbs. pressure—and is ideal for medium and large lawns and gardens.

Price $10.00; Denver and West $10.75

The Giant Rain King

For big lawns, estates, parks, etc. S 4 feet tall with four nozzles, all quick to any Rain King sprinkling action. metal pads on legs save undergrow big capacity sprinkler. Rain King is with bronze bearings, *free from pres*

Price $12.50; Denver and West $14.5

We can almost feel the grass exhaling under our feet. And we reward it with a light sprinkle of cool water. What pure, simple pleasure! And we can take pride in knowing that we're doing something good for the lawn.

Or are we? Probably not.

Perhaps our well-intentioned watering is doing some good—for us, by providing some quiet quality time alone with our lawns. But chances are it's not really helping the grass. In fact, it's probably hurting it. (As they say: You always hurt the one you love.)

Sure, grass needs water, and lots of it. To grow vigorously, an established lawn requires, on the average, about an inch of water per week. That may not sound like much, but if your hose is providing 10 gallons a minute, it would take more than 40 hours with a hose in hand to water a one-acre lawn. By that time your arm would be aching and sprinkling would have lost much of its romance.

But to give the lawn less water—to sprinkle rather than soak—causes problems. Regular light sprinklings encourage the grass roots to stay near the surface. Consequently, if that sprinkling stops, if the supply is cut off—due to restrictions, vacations, or just plain laziness—the grass will not be equipped to dig deep into the soil to find water. Thus it will become more susceptible to drought, disease, and insect stress.

Fortunately, we don't have to handle all the watering ourselves. Unless it's freshly sown or newly sodded, the lawn can do a remarkable job of taking care of itself. In temperate regions of the country, where

DROUGHT RESISTANCE OF GRASSES

The best way to reduce your watering time is to plant drought-resistant grasses. Here are some of the best species:

MOST DROUGHT RESISTANT

Bermudagrass

Zoysiagrass

Buffalograss

Tall fescue

Fine fescue

MODERATELY DROUGHT RESISTANT

Kentucky bluegrass

Perennial ryegrass

St. Augustinegrass

Bahiagrass

➤ Beneath a typical patch of turf, there are hundreds of thousands of miles of grass roots, tapping into subsurface moisture, pumping that welcome water up through the stems to the leaves, where it is ultimately released as water vapor, cooling the surrounding air. A thick carpet of turf also prevents erosion.

rainfall is adequate and where turf is well adapted, nature takes care of the bulk of the watering most of the year. And when rain doesn't fall regularly, there's a miraculous reservoir system that can store water for long periods of time. It's called soil. A good, rich soil can hold enormous amounts of water, where the roots of the grass plants can access it as needed.

Soil varies widely in how much water it can hold, depending on texture and composition. A heavy clay soil, for example, will hold three times as much moisture as a sandy soil. A foot-deep section of clay can hold $2\frac{1}{2}$ inches of water—enough to carry a lawn through two and a half weeks without rain. The same size section of sand, however, will hold only $\frac{3}{4}$ of an inch of water—less than a week's worth of moisture.

NO JOB for a woman?
What do you think?

"NO JOB," says CHESTER H. SMITH of Whittier, Calif. *"I don't feel right about letting my wife do outdoor work like sprinkling the lawn. Besides it's good for me, keeps my waistline down. And I save money by buying 'Garden Club' hose."*

"MY JOB," says Mrs. VIRGINIA SOWDER of Los Angeles, Calif. *"I enjoy working in my garden—and healthy exercise is just as good for me as for my husband. Koroseal hose is so light even 7-year-old Carol helps me carry it around."*

IF you're on the lady's side of this debate, better get Koroseal. It never needs to be drained, can be left out in the sun for years with no more harm than a little dulling of its bright red or green. *And it's so light a child can handle it!*

GUARANTEED 10 YEARS!

Even dragging it over rough, concrete won't hurt Koroseal. It's guaranteed by B. F. Goodrich for *10 years.*

Get the economical 75-foot length that reaches every part of most home-sites. Koroseal garden hose costs only $9.35 for 50 feet or $13.20 for 75 feet.

If you're the man of the house and none of this nonsense about letting the missus do *your* work—"Garden Club" is your buy. It's light enough for you to haul around (lighter, in fact, than most rubber hose) and it saves you $1.40 on 50 feet. Attractive sage green color.

Garden Club and Koroseal Garden Hose are in department and hardware stores now. Both are guaranteed for 10 years by B. F. Goodrich. *Look for the label. The B. F. Goodrich Company, Industrial and General Products Division, Akron, Ohio.*

(Koroseal—Trade Mark—Reg. U. S. Pat. Off.)

Koroseal
**GARDEN HOSE
BY
B.F.Goodrich**

This ad for men only

MEN should buy the garden hose—but keeping the women very much in mind. If you do it right you can sell them the idea of doing more outdoor work *and liking it.*

If your wife never uses the hose maybe you don't need Koroseal. It costs a little more—but only $9.80 for 50 feet and makes up for it by being so easy to handle. It is *guaranteed to last ten years.*

"Garden Club", also made by B. F. Goodrich, and guaranteed 10 years, is lighter than most rubber hose, a wonderful value.

But Koroseal is a third lighter still (weighs only half as much as some hose). It's *clean;* the surface has a high polish, doesn't hold dirt. No need to drain it or lug it in either. Leave it out all year round if you want to. Its brilliant colors may fade a little, but neither sun nor air will weaken it.

Look for the label. Every length is plainly marked. Be sure you see the name to be sure you're getting the real thing. *The B. F. Goodrich Company, Industrial & General Products Division, Akron, Ohio.*

Koroseal—Trade Mark—Reg. U. S. Pat. Off.

Koroseal
**GARDEN HOSE
BY
B.F.Goodrich**

◄ Maybe we men weren't willing to let women in on the pleasures of lawn mowing in the 1950s, but by then, we could at least think about allowing them to share in the joys of watering the lawn. As lightweight plastics replaced heavy rubber in the manufacturing of hoses, the job became something that even ladies could handle.

To cover a one-acre lawn with an inch-thick blanket of water would require 27,144 gallons. That's enough to fill a 20-by-30-foot swimming pond to a depth of 6 feet. That's over 200,000 pounds of water. And it's just a week's ration for the lawn.

So the secret of good watering is to think not of watering the plants but of filling the reservoir with water so that the roots can get to it. Grass plants are not dumb. Like us, they won't work any harder than they have to. If the roots grow accustomed to a regular sprinkling of water that barely soaks through the soil surface, then they will do most of their growing near the surface. However, if regular heavy watering seeps deep into the soil, the roots will follow. And in times of drought, as the level of water in the soil falls, the roots will have pushed deep enough to extract all available water.

Some grasses are better than others at plying the soil for moisture. The ability to go get water varies considerably from species to species, depending to a large degree on the ability to grow roots. Bentgrasses are the worst, because their roots are the shortest, only 1 to 8 inches long. That's why golf course superintendents turn on the sprinklers on the bent grass green every morning. By comparison, bluegrass, ryegrass, red fescue, and St. Augustinegrass roots may delve as deep as 18 inches. But that's nothing compared to tall fescue, Bermudagrass, and zoysiagrass, which may send their roots as deep as 5 feet into the soil.

So what's the best way to get water to the roots? Not with a hose in hand but with a sprinkler.

THE SPIRITUAL LAWN OF PLAY

As we push the mower across the lawn, we travel backward, deeper into the past. We conjure up memories that we rarely have the time or permission to otherwise think about, except perhaps on holidays or birthdays or other family gatherings. But if we allow ourselves to succumb to the monotony of the task, the roar of the machine, the magic of the lawn, and let go of where we are, we feel the wisp of memory rise. *(Note: The Whistle-While-You-Work Society advises you to always keep two hands on the handlebars. Do not operate power machinery while under the influence of alcoholic beverages, or while under the sway of nostalgia. Do not allow yourself to be lulled into a trance.)*

As we mow inward, we become younger. We shed our older, outer, responsible selves, much as the grass plant gives up its older growth when it's mown.

As we men—all right, women too—grow older, our lives are taken over by responsibilities. But the lawn is a reminder of the fields of play of our childhood. The lawn is forever linked with the games of our youth. Baseball, football, soccer are all played on grass. While spending a Saturday behind the mower, we often find ourselves daydreaming about summer evenings chasing down a ball or running as fast as we can.

Even as adults we feel goose bumps at the first sight of the sparkling green outfield of Yankee Stadium or Fenway Park as we emerge from beneath the stands into the sunlight. As we walk the fairway of a golf course, we can feel a childlike joy bubbling up from beneath our feet. And perhaps for a moment we recognize that it is, after all, a game played on grass. On the lawn we hold on with all of our strength to those memories. For all the work that we invest in the lawn, that patch of grass is also virtually the only place left where we are allowed to play, to put on shorts and ugly shirts and barbecue and putter—or just sit.

SPRINKLER SPEAK

You don't have to be a hydraulic engineer to pick a sprinkler, but it helps if you can talk the talk with the sales clerk and decipher the numbers on the sprinkler box. Here are four terms commonly used to rate the performance of a sprinkler:

➤ **DISTRIBUTION PATTERN** indicates the shape of the coverage area of the sprinkler. Patterns range from circles and semicircles to squares and rectangles. Some sprinklers are adjustable to allow for different-shaped patterns. The best pattern for you is the one that conforms to the shape of your lawn.

➤ **THROW RADIUS** denotes the maximum distance covered by the sprinkler. It may range from 25 to 75 feet. The longer the throw radius, the more area the sprinkler covers, and so the less often you have to move it.

➤ **FLOW RATE,** or average precipitation rate, is a measure of the amount of water put down by the sprinkler in one hour. It may range from ¼ inch per hour to nearly 1 inch per hour. In most cases the lower the flow rate, the better, because a low flow rate allows time for the water to soak into the soil.

➤ **UNIFORMITY** may be the most critical consideration. It is a comparative measure of how much water is dropped at various points along the throw radius. The best sprinklers are the most uniform.

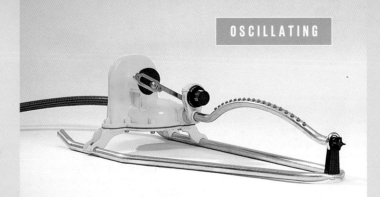

OSCILLATING

SPRINKLER SPECS

There are six basic types of lawn sprinklers: fixed, revolving, traveling, oscillating, impulse, and in-ground. They vary considerably in their ability to do the job.

How well sprinklers measure up in these qualities depends primarily on their design. Each of the six categories of sprinklers has its own strengths and weaknesses.

➤ **FIXED SPRINKLERS** offer the advantage of low price and simplicity. They're inexpensive, and they have no moving parts. Water simply shoots out of pinholes in the nozzle. Some models are adjustable; you can twist the head for different distribution patterns: square, rectangle, circle, semicircle, and so on. Even though they're cheap, fixed sprinklers are hardly worth the cost. They generally have the shortest throw radius of all sprinklers, and they don't soak the area uniformly. They tend to leak around the head so that most of the water falls within a couple of feet of the sprinkler.

➤ **REVOLVING SPRINKLERS** have a rotating arm that spins around at a dizzying rate, shooting water from a nozzle at each end of the arm. These are the sprinklers that kids love to run through in the summer. They're good for that but not much else. Their throw radius is low, and uniformity is very poor. Most of the water falls in puddles directly around the base.

➤ **TRAVELING SPRINKLERS** offer an interesting spin on lawn irrigation. These are revolving sprinklers mounted on a traveling base that usually resembles a miniature tractor. They're generally

FIXED

IMPULSE

expensive and well made, so they offer more uniformity than cheap revolving sprinklers. And because they travel, following the hose that you lay out across the lawn, they eliminate the basic problem of low throw radius. Besides, they're fun. They make watering the lawn like playing farm.

➤ **OSCILLATING SPRINKLERS** are the most common lawn sprinklers, in no small part because their rectangular pattern covers standard rectangular suburban lawns so well. Drive through a development on a summer evening, and you'll see sprinkler after sprinkler methodically shooting up its fan of water, the arm rocking back and forth like a metronome timing the rhythm of the suburbs, pausing at its apex as if to gather strength and resolve, then back again. For the most part, this type of sprinkler is a good choice. Most models of this type have uniform distribution patterns and a decent throw radius. However, the least expensive units show a serious lack of uniformity: They drop more moisture on the downside of their swing, resulting in puddles that can give rise to disease, weeds, and generally unhealthy turf.

➤ **IMPULSE SPRINKLERS** are modeled after agricultural sprinklers. A powerful jet of water shoots from a nozzle, then is broken up into droplets by a spring-loaded arm. The impact causes the nozzle to revolve in a circle. These sprinklers generally have a good throw radius, and in tests they've shown the greatest uniformity of all sprinklers, though they sometimes leave puddles near the base of the sprinkler.

➤ **IN-GROUND SPRINKLERS** are best suited for large lawns in arid regions, where lawns really can't grow without supplemental water. They're expensive to purchase and difficult to install—with lines running underground and pop-up sprinkler heads rigged to a timer. The heads, which are situated to give thorough coverage, may be either fixed or revolving. They're installed in a pattern that ensures complete coverage, so throw radius is not a question and uniformity is generally good.

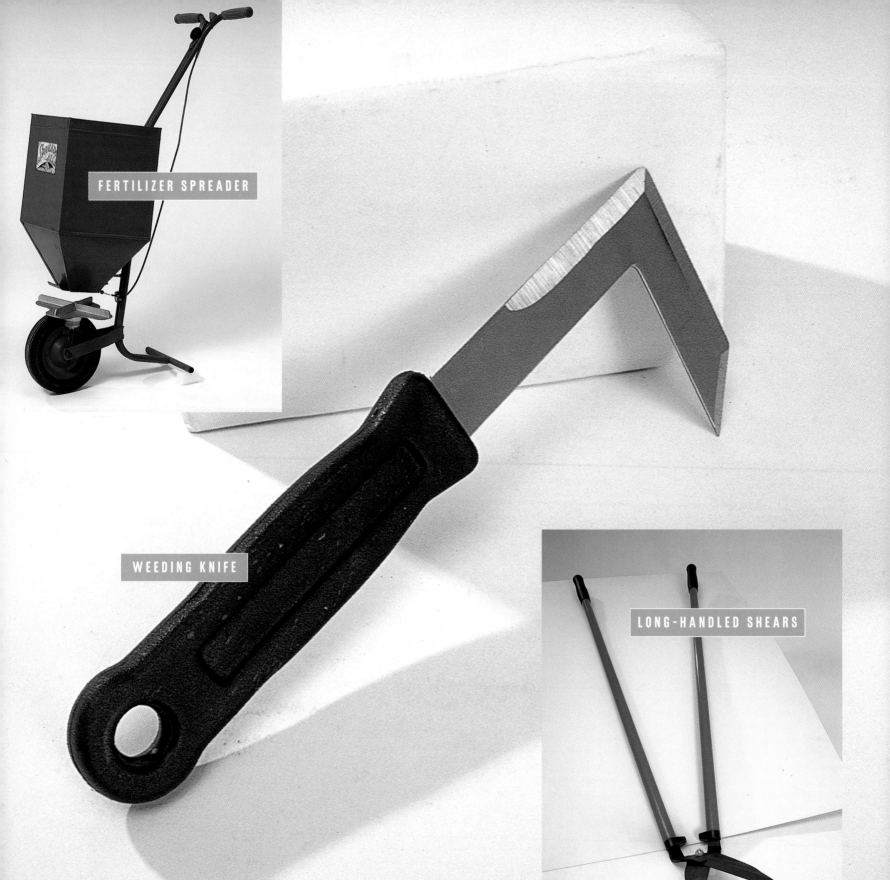

FERTILIZER SPREADER

WEEDING KNIFE

LONG-HANDLED SHEARS

THE LAWN OWNER'S TOOL KIT

Lawn care is not brain surgery, and you don't need a shed full of specialized tools to get it done. But there are a few necessary implements and supplies:

LAWN MOWER
It seems like a no-brainer. You can't have a lawn without something to mow it with, and scythes, weed whips, and string trimmers just won't do the job. Besides cutting the grass, though, the right lawn mower can also fight weeds and help to feed the grass.

METAL RAKE
You'll find a sturdy rake indispensable for preparing new ground to replant the lawn, for removing thatch, for overseeding, for top-dressing with organic matter, and for something to lean on while chatting with the neighbors.

HAND AERATOR
Because the lawn is never turned over and the soil beneath it is never tilled or plowed, it tends to become compacted, slowing the penetration of moisture, fertilizer, and the roots themselves. With a hand aerator you can loosen and rejuvenate the soil without disturbing the lawn.

HAND WEEDER
Every lawn has weeds. You can ignore them, you can spray them, or you can take them on one by one with a long-handled lawn-weeding tool. The good ones will remove the weeds, root and all, so that there is no regrowth.

FERTILIZER SPREADER
Though lawns may not require frequent fertilization, they'll need a feeding at least once a year. The fertilizer must be applied uniformly to avoid uneven growth and stress problems. A drop spreader will do the job better than a cyclone-type spreader.

TAPE MEASURE
Instructions for mowing, feeding, watering, and general lawn maintenance all involve measurements: Mow at a certain height, apply a certain amount per 1,000 square feet. You'll need to measure your turf to get it right.

LAWN SHEARS
No matter how large or small your lawn, and whatever its shape or design, there will be areas that your lawn mower can't get to. A pair of lawn shears, preferably long-handled, will help you keep your lawn trim.

NOTEBOOK
Just as you keep a journal for your flower or vegetable garden, you should maintain a lawn diary, making note of frequency of mowing, watering, fertilizing, and so on.

SHARP SPADE
You'll find this basic tool useful for digging out patches of weeds, edging the lawn, replacing patches of sod, and many more lawn chores.

SPRINKLER
It's inevitable: At some point your lawn is going to be dying for a drink, and you'll need a sprinkler to deliver the water. Choose one with a high throw radius and low flow rate. (See page 106 for more details.)

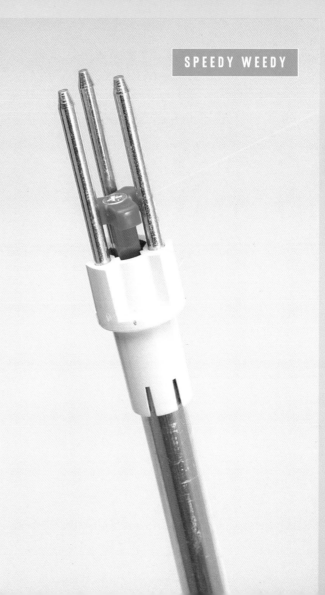

SPEEDY WEEDY

WATER CYCLING

In the best of cases you can turn on the sprinkler, walk away, and return in an hour or two to find the lawn thoroughly watered with no runoff or puddles. If the flow rate of your sprinkler matches the infiltration rate of your soil, that's what will happen. But more often than not, the sprinkler will deliver water at a rate faster than the ground can absorb it, and the water will run off. That results in wasted water, puddles, and ultimately damage to your lawn. That's when you have to resort to water cycling.

Suppose your lawn is growing in loamy soil (we should all be so lucky), which typically has an infiltration rate of about $\frac{1}{4}$ inch per hour, and you're using a sprinkler with a flow rate of one inch per hour. If you run the sprinkler for an hour, you've dispensed the required inch of water, but the soil has

absorbed only $\frac{1}{4}$ inch in that time. The rest is wasted. You could switch to a sprinkler with a lower flow rate or adjust your sprinkling schedule. Run that sprinkler just fifteen minutes at a time and leave it off for forty-five minutes. That way you've put down $\frac{1}{4}$ inch in an hour—just what the soil can accept. After one hour, run the sprinkler again for fifteen minutes. Repeat this cycle for a total of four times and you've put down the required amount.

That, of course, requires some commitment and a fair amount of running back and forth to the faucet. Instead, you can install a simple timer that will do the job for you.

Once you have your new water toy, the hardest part may be resisting the temptation to play with it too much. Discretion and moderation are required. In arid regions of the country, lawns do need to be watered weekly. But in most Northern areas, you should water only when the grass really needs it. It will let you know. Grass wilts when it approaches dehydration. The blades turn from green to a dull gray. The plants lack springiness; the blades will lie flat rather than bounce back in your footsteps after you walk across the lawn. That's the time to water.

Even without water, most Northern grasses have a defense mechanism. They won't die during drought but will slip into dormancy, turn brown, and stop growing. But when rains resume, they'll green up almost immediately and spring back to life.

Maybe the lawn doesn't have to be green all the

> Impulse sprinklers are the water-delivery method of choice for farms, golf courses, and research centers because of their superior uniformity and throw radius.

SOIL INFILTRATION RATES

Soils vary considerably in their ability to soak up moisture. Water travels quickly through sand, for example, but penetrates clay slowly. The type of soil under your lawn should influence your choice of sprinkler. The flow rate of a sprinkler should not exceed the infiltration rates of the soil. Here are the infiltration rates for several types of soil.

Soil Texture	Inches/Hour
clay	0.1
clay loam	0.15
loam	0.25
sandy loam	0.5
sand	1.0

time. Perhaps it should be allowed to react to the weather and the seasons. Consider letting the grass fend for itself. Allow the lawn to lose some of its luster during the dog days of summer. Let it slow down and catch its breath, as you do the same. And when the grass regains its luster in the autumn, you can rejoice in its resurrection. Welcome it back, and enjoy one last rush of mowing and tending before winter shuts it all down. Because once you turn on that faucet, you're opening the floodgates and setting forces into motion that can't be reversed. In the process you're making more work for yourself. More water often means more weeds, sometimes more disease, and always more mowing. In the end you're making the lawn more dependent on you and taking on responsibility. And don't you have enough of that?

6 PLANTS OUT OF PLACE

IF THERE'S ANYTHING that casts a pall over the lawn, it's weeds. Damned dandelions—those perversely cheery yellow flowers—breaking out suddenly like acne on the face of a teenager getting ready for the prom. If there's anything that makes us gnash our teeth while we're trying to enjoy our turf, it's weeds. Crabgrass—insidious impostor snaking through the grass. If there's anything that interrupts our revelry, it's weeds. Purslane, plantain, nimbleweed, and wood sorrel—their names sputter from our lips like curses. Their very existence nags us like chores undone. Some say weeds are a sign of soil deficiencies, but when they overrun the lawn, they feel like signs of our own deficiencies.

Dandelions especially gall us, because they are a constant reminder of our loss of innocence. As children we love them. We're transfixed by their magical overnight appearance. We wake one morning in May to discover that, out of nowhere, the lawn has been transformed into a sea of gold. We pick them for chains and crowns and games. We yank them by the handful and arrange them into bouquets that fill our little fists. And

◄ From its thick leathery leaves to its spindly stalk and ugly seed head, plantain is one of the worst lawn leaves.

we proudly present them to our parents, who cannot quite hide their disdain for these weeds. Of course, they feign delight. But somehow we see through it. And we begin to wonder: What's wrong with dandelions? What is wrong with us for being so totally seduced by them? The next morning the flowers droop in a jelly jar. That's the morning of our rude awakening, when we begin to recognize that all that appears bountiful and beautiful is not necessarily so.

In our adult dreams, our lawns are wide, long, green, and spotless. They're like putting greens, Astroturf outfields, pool tables. Botanically, we expect our lawns to be exclusive societies where only turf grass is admitted. We want our lawns to be grass and nothing but grass as far as the eye can see. In those lawns in our minds, there are no surprises, no disappointments.

But reality rarely matches our dreams. Weeds insinuate themselves into the lawn, creeping in like doubts. They mock and humble us, reminding us with every sprout, leaf, and flower that we cannot exert complete control over this turf of ours. They remind us that nature is stronger than we are, because when it comes right down to it, weeds are more natural than turf. After all, turf grass is the invader. Weeds are the local resistance.

Their seeds are carried on the wind. They travel on the soles of our shoes, or stuck to the fur of animals. But mostly those seeds are in the soil, waiting. . . . With every opportunity, every ray of light, every drop of water, every spot of bare soil, they'll germinate and grow. And we engage in the Sisyphean task of trying to annihilate them.

This obsession with weeds in the lawn is a late-twentieth-century phenomenon. Until the middle of the century, weeds were pretty much accepted in lawns. They were met with a shrug rather than a curse. Yes, farmers and gardeners have always hoed, chopped, burned, and pulled weeds from farms and gardens, but the lawn is different. The thickly knitted mat of grasses that covers virtually every inch of ground makes it more difficult to gain a purchase on the weeds and remove them.

◄ Ground ivy, a member of the mint family, was originally introduced to this country as a ground cover. Since then it has conquered many a lawn with its creeping habit.
► Dandelion is, like ground ivy, a cool season weed that spreads via both its root and the thousands of puffball seeds it sends into the air.

Typically, the top 6-inch layer of 1,000 square feet of soil will contain up to 40 million weed seeds. That's more than 5,000 seeds per square foot.

DANDELION PATROL

Dandelions are the bane of lawn-lovers. They are highly visible, tenacious, and prolific. They owe the latter qualities to their long, sturdy taproot that can dig as much as 1 foot into the ground. Chop them, pull them, dig them, but if the bulk of the root remains, the plant will spring back with renewed vigor. However, if you can extract that taproot, just 4 or 5 inches of it, chances are you've passed the death sentence on that plant. You can kill dandelions by cutting them too, but it requires persistence. In spring use long-handled shears to snip off the stems and leaves as close to the ground as possible. When the roots respond by sending up new shoots, clip them as well. Keep at it, and after five or six clippings, the root will have exhausted its reserves and the plant will die.

◄ Crabgrass likes the heat. This summer annual spreads like wildfire through thin lawns, especially those that are mowed too low and sprinkled too often. ➤ Plantain (top) is a perennial lawn weed and a perennial problem in underfertilized turf. Purslane (bottom) is a relative of the flowering ornamental portulaca. Some say its young leaves are tasty in a salad. Most say it doesn't belong in the lawn.

A weed-free lawn was not desirable until it was possible. And it was not truly possible until the advent of chemical weed-killers. Just as strike-outs and Wite-Out were allowed on papers until we had computers, four television channels were fine until we had cable, black and white was okay until we had color, so weeds were an acceptable element of the lawns until we had weed-killers.

Sure, weeds were anathema in some cases. On golf greens a single stalk of plantain could come between a par and a bogie. So during the Great Depression, men and children found work as weed-pulling gangs on golf courses. Early in the morning you could find them crawling over the greens and picking and pulling weeds by hand. In the case of stubborn weeds that spread by roots and rhizomes, the weeders had to roll back patches of the sod and extract the roots and rhizomes from the soil beneath the grass.

THE UNWINNABLE WAR

In time there were attempts to replace the sharp tools and human sweat with witches' brews of chemical compounds. Table salt, sulfuric acid, and sulfate of ammonia were all used as weed-killers. One common recommendation was to douse dandelions with kerosene. It killed them, yes, but it poisoned the soil and surrounding plants as well. Others offered instructions for using an ice pick to insert battery acid into the crown of plantain plants.

◄ Speedwell is another ornamental plant, a veronica relative that has become a lawn weed. It thrives in cool, moist soils and thin turf. ► Curly dock is a large, warm-season perennial that appears in lawns during summer, when the grass is stressed by heat and drought.

In the 1930s there were many experiments using arsenic compounds to kill weeds on golf courses and in lawns. In the 1940s one lawn-supply company began experimenting with organic mercury as an herbicide. It sent unmarked samples of a dry mercury formulation to homeowners and had them spread it on their lawns with a spreader. It worked, and by 1950 the company was recommending applications of their mercury product every twenty-one days, calling it "as essential as food in lawn growing."

But mercury and all those other solutions were about to be rendered obsolete by a new miracle compound. In 1943 the United States Army paid $3,500 to the University of Chicago to conduct herbicide research. The research was then handed over to the Special Projects Division of the Chemical Warfare Service, which synthesized and tested the growth hormone compound 2,4-dichlorophenoxy acetic acid. In tests on home lawns, golf courses, and even the White House lawn, researchers found that this chemical, by now known as 2,4-D, effectively killed dandelions and other broad-leaved plants without harming the surrounding grass. This was a major breakthrough: the first practical selective herbicide ever. Originally the plan was to use this chemical to kill the crops in farm fields of the enemy, but when the war ended and the veil of secrecy was lifted, private industry rushed to embrace this new miracle chemical. By 1945 the American Chemical Paint Company had patented and begun marketing 2,4-D

as Weedone. Farmers, gardeners, and homeowners were amazed at its selective property. Nearly 100,000 pounds of the chemical were produced in 1945. That rose to 5 million pounds in 1946 and 36 million pounds in 1960. By the 1990s, production figures approached 50 million pounds per year.

This chemical, 2,4-D (which was eventually combined with 2,4,5-T to make Agent Orange) revolutionized lawn care and, by extension, transformed the lawn itself. Suddenly it was theoretically possible to have a weed-free lawn without struggling. And once it was possible, it was desirable.

Many, many other herbicides followed 2,4-D onto the market. Today Americans spend more than $200 million to apply more than 27 million pounds of herbicide-active ingredients on their lawns every year. (The active ingredient is only a small fraction of total weight.) We've got preemergence, postemergence, selective, broad-spectrum, granular, powdered, and liquid herbicides. For virtually every weed, we've got a weed-killer. And you know what? We've still got weeds. We're not winning the war. It's a stalemate.

The dollars spent are just part of the cost. Even if you believe that the health hazards of herbicides are just New Age tree-hugging hooey; even if you dismiss the studies that show that farmers who use 2,4-D have a higher risk of contracting non-Hodgkin's lymphoma or those that show that dogs whose owners use 2,4-D are more likely to have

GIVE WEEDS AN INCH...

If there's a bare spot in the lawn, you can bet that weeds will take advantage of it and move in before the turf grass does. So one of your greatest weed-fighting tools is a bag of grass seed. Keep one on hand, and whenever you spot a bare patch in the lawn, grab the bag and reseed.

First rough up the soil with a rake to give the seed a good chance to gain purchase. Spread the seed, then top-dress with topsoil, sand, or sifted compost. Keep the area moist until the grass emerges.

Resodding is even more foolproof. Set aside a small patch in the vegetable garden or flower bed and sow it thickly with a premium grass seed. Keep it well mowed and watered, and when you need to cover bare patches you can use a spade or even a knife or garden machete to carve out a small piece of sod to use. After removing the sod, reseed your sod bed for further use and to keep the weeds from invading it.

canine leukemia; even if you ignore groundwater pollution, it's difficult to dismiss the deleterious effects that herbicides have on the soil and, by extension, the grass that grows in it. Because, simply, there's no denying that herbicides are toxins. They disrupt the microorganisms of the soil that feed and protect the plants growing in it.

Forget all that, and the larger questions remains: Do we really need these chemicals? Do we need to spend money and time applying toxins to our yards? Must we hire those chemical lawn-care services and submit to the indignity of little warning signs on our front lawns?

Probably not. Because resorting to quick-fix chemicals artificializes our relationship with the lawn. It removes us from the lawn. Anytime you have to put on rubber gloves and a mask, it's not puttering anymore. It's serious business. And the lawn should be the one place that provides sanctuary from the serious.

◄ Red chickweed creeps into shady, moist areas of the lawn and covers the ground with its rooting stems. But it doesn't dig in deeply, and so it can be pulled out without too much trouble.

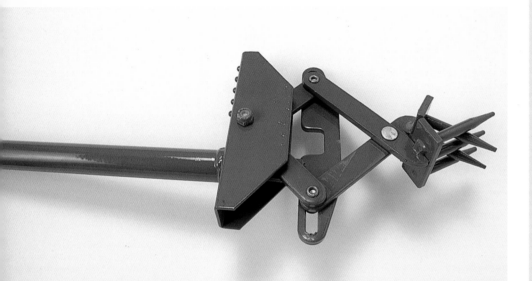

Not a medieval implement of torture but a lawn-weeding tool, the jaws of the Back Savr Easy Weeder are designed to extract deep-rooted weeds such as dandelions.
We get carried away when we get our hands on a lawn mower, as we're tempted to mow the grass to within an inch of its life, but mowing high makes the grass healthier and helps to vanquish crabgrass and other weeds.

Since the dawning of the age of herbicides, the lawn has strayed ever further from simple nature. It has become less of a garden. When we use weed-killers, we don't have to learn about our lawns or the weeds that inhabit it. We don't have to figure out how to manage them. Controlling weeds with guile and muscle has become a forgotten art.

But weeds, even lawn weeds, can be managed without chemicals. How? What about weeding them? Just as you would if weeds cropped up in the flower bed or vegetable patch. Granted, many lawn weeds are firmly entrenched in the turf, but they can be extracted without hours of grubbing along on your hands and knees. You'd be amazed at how quickly you can clear a 1,000-foot lawn of dandelions, especially if you employ a specialized long-handled lawn-weeding tool. There are plenty of them on the market, Rube Goldberg–like contrap-

MOW THOSE WEEDS AWAY

One of your best weeding tools is the lawn mower itself, if you mow properly, which almost always means mowing high.

High mowing has several advantages. First, it makes for healthier turf. The grass has more surface area to collect sunlight and manufacture energy, and taller plants have deeper roots that can dig for water and nutrients. Finally, tall grass shades the ground to inhibit the germination and growth of many weeds.

In fact, a study at the University of Rhode Island (URI) showed that mowing a bluegrass lawn at the proper height can virtually eliminate crabgrass over five years.

Researchers at URI started with two identical plots, both infested with crabgrass—up to one third of the area was covered with this weed. They mowed one plot low, at 1¼ inches. By the third year, crabgrass had taken over that plot and covered more than half the ground. But in the second plot, mowed at 2¼ inches, the crabgrass covered only 7 percent of the ground by the end of the fifth year.

A similar study at the University of Maryland demonstrated that high mowing works to control a wide range of weeds. There researchers started with two identical 100-square-foot plots of lawn. They kept one mowed at 1½ inches tall and kept the other mowed at 2½ inches tall. After two years, they counted fifty-three weeds in the low-mowed lawn, but only eight in the high-mowed lawn.

High mowing alone won't eradicate every weed, but, in general, it's an effective strategy against low-growing, prostrate weeds such as annual bluegrass, speedwell, witchgrass, crabgrass, and nut sedge.

WILD ONION

PLANTAIN

A ROGUES' GALLERY

COLTSFOOT

DOCK

INDIAN STRAWBERRY

QUACKGRASS

OF WEEDS

DANDELION

HENBIT

CHICKWEED

CRABGRASS

tions with sharp teeth and snapping jaws. They have their own playful appeal—guaranteed to amaze and intrigue your neighbors. Stroll around your lawn with a weed popper in the evening, and before long you'll attract a crowd of the curious. Before you know it, they'll be asking, "Hey, can I try that?" And you can stand back as the Tom-Sawyer-whitewashing-the-fence effect takes hold.

The best way to deal with weeds is to make sure they don't get a toehold in the grass. They say that the best weed control is a thick, healthy stand of turf, and the sod fields at Fairwood Turf Farms are living proof that it's true.

LESSONS FROM A SOD FARM

The lawn out behind Eugene Roberts's house in Glenn Dale, Maryland, covers several acres. And it's virtually weed-free. It has to be. His backyard is a sod farm, or at least part of the Fairwood Turf Farms —and it is required by law to be virtually weed-free.

The house sits in the midst of a three-hundred-year-old farm that's crisscrossed with dirt roads that climb and wind around rolling hills dotted with thick stands of mature oak trees. If you were to climb one of those trees and look east, you'd be able to see the Washington Monument, only fourteen miles away.

This family farm had been in tobacco for some three hundred years, but when Roberts's father,

BROADLEAF PLANTAIN

ANNUAL BLUEGRASS

Eugene Sr., took over in 1939, he converted the land to general farming, raising some vegetables, a little grain, and a few cattle. Most of the land was turned over to pasture.

It was then, and is now, a beautiful farm. "Dad was an ardent conservationist," says Roberts. "He worked hard to bring the soil back. In 1952 the farm won the county's greener pasture contest, and the next year it won the state award."

The farm attracted notice from passersby even then. At the time the suburbs around Washington were booming. Houses were going up in a hurry, and they needed lawns by the yard.

Contractors driving by couldn't help but cast a covetous eye at the farm. They knew that lawns were what made their houses into homes. Surrounded by lawns, the new developments took on a soft green tint. Only in the presence of a lawn could buyers imagine picnics, ball games, and lazy afternoons. It was the lawn that would finish the home and make it feel welcoming and safe.

Of course, the contractors were impatient. They needed a carpet of grass that they could just roll out in a day like a rug. They needed sod. And they saw acres and acres of it just lying there. So one day in 1955 an enterprising contractor stopped by Fairwood Farms with a proposition: Would they be willing to sell off the pasture piece by piece? Though it was

127

WHIPPING WEEDS

Even if you don't care to outmuscle the weeds, you can outwit them through cultural controls. Weeds are a lot like garden plants. (Actually, many lawn weeds—violets, veronica, speedwell—*are* garden plants.) And they have their own preferred growing conditions. They can be forced out of the lawn by denying them what they want, whether it's sun, shade, moisture, and so on. But weeds are not a monolithic enemy. Like turf grasses, they can be divided into many types, each with different characteristics.

COOL-SEASON ANNUALS

Cool-season annuals such as chickweed, speedwell, knotweed, and henbit are especially troublesome. They germinate and grow vigorously when the weather is cool—spring in the North or winter in the South. In the North, spring is just when turf grass is getting started, so weeds engage in direct competition with the grass, and they often win. And in the South, the warm-season grasses are just lazily cracking out of dormancy in winter, so the cool-season weeds have a leg up on them. There are some techniques, however, for eliminating these plants:

➤ Do not fertilize the Northern lawn in spring or the Southern lawn in winter, when cool-season weeds will take advantage of the food and grow even more vigorously.

➤ Mow the Northern lawn high in spring and the Southern lawn high in winter and spring.

➤ In summer, use a metal garden rake to pull out the creeping stems of the weeds.

COOL-SEASON PERENNIALS

Clover, speedwell, ground ivy, violets, plantain, dandelions, and other cool-season perennials are also at their best in spring. Their control is the same on both Northern and Southern lawns:

➤ Rake the lawn early in the spring with a metal garden rake to raise the creeping stems of the weeds.

➤ Mow the grass low after raking.

➤ Collect and dispose of the clippings to remove the stems of the weeds so they can't root in the soil.

WARM-SEASON ANNUALS

These weeds, including purslane, spurge, wood sorrel, and crabgrass, like the heat. They compete vigorously against cool-season grasses in summer, when grasses are edging toward dormancy.

➤ Refrain from feeding and watering the lawn in summer.

➤ Mow at the recommended height, but use a bagger to collect clippings while the weed seed heads are present.

WARM-SEASON PERENNIALS

These are mainly grassy weeds like nut sedge or nimbleweed and warm-season grasses that are out of place in cool-season lawns. They spread when cool-season turf grasses are stressed and struggling in the heat.

➤ Use a weeding tool to remove clumps of these weeds, root, rhizome, and all.

➤ Mow high to lessen the stress on desirable grasses.

None of these techniques offers the quick fix that chemicals do, but over time they will make the lawn less hospitable for weeds and gradually get rid of most of them. In the meantime we need to extract the seed of lawn perfectionism from our minds. Maybe the best weed-control tool is your mind's eye. Weedy is in the eye of the beholder. There may be no truer horticultural observation than "A weed is a plant out of place." Let's go back to an earlier time, when men were men and lawns were weedy, and we didn't care.

America's
3 Great Gardening Aids!

SEE WHAT A BEAUTIFUL DIFFERENCE THEY MAKE!
PRESENTED BY SWIFT & COMPANY

VIGORO*

New process Vigoro makes grass greener —goes ⅓ further—nourishes longer than ever before. So complete, so perfectly balanced—actual tests show it makes even common sand grow grass like finest golf course soil! Apply at the rate of 3 lbs. per 100 square feet. Ideal for flowers, trees, shrubs, vegetables, too!

There is only one Vigoro . . . the trade-mark for Swift & Company's complete, balanced plant food.

End-o-Pest

Stop pest troubles before they start— with all-purpose End-o-Pest! Supplies the pest protection every garden needs because it controls chewing and sucking insects and fungus diseases . . . the 3 major types. Ready-mixed. Ideal for flowers, trees, shrubs and edible fruits and vegetables as well.

End-o-Weed

Weed your whole lawn in less than one hour! Just dilute End-o-Weed with water and apply. Kills over 100 varieties of weeds—leaves, roots and all—without harming ordinary lawn grass. Eight ounces treat 2,000 sq. ft.

◄ Every eighteen months, Eugene Roberts and his crew harvest the sod at Fairwood Turf Farms and start all over again. Virtually all the sod is composed of a mix of 10 percent Kentucky bluegrass and 90 percent turf-type tall fescue. Growing fast and thick, it crowds out the weeds so that herbicides are hardly needed at all.

➤ The sod is harvested with a ¹⁄₂-inch-thick layer of roots attached, then rolled onto pallets for delivery.

rough pasture, mainly orchardgrass, a little blue-grass, and clover, it was still green.

Roberts saw a chance to supplement his income and agreed. Soon there were trucks lining up at the gate, fifteen to twenty of them a day. They would harvest sod with their little cutters and roll it up by hand. In his own way, Roberts was reprising the early days of the lawn, when "turves" were dug from pasture and replanted around houses.

In the mid-'60s, he converted the farm to 100 percent turf grass. Every inch of the farm, hill and valley, was seeded, mowed, and fertilized. In that time turf grass was more valuable than grain, vegetables, or livestock.

The business grew as fast as a bluegrass lawn in May. These days the younger Roberts employs a crew of more than a dozen men to harvest and install hundreds of acres of sod virtually year round. And

131

WHAT ABOUT BUGS?

When it comes to keeping the lawn in top shape, insects are the least of our worries. Sure, there are turf pests, such as chinch bugs, sod webworms, mole crickets, and others, but they rarely appear in numbers large enough to damage a lawn. If they do show up, it's usually a sign that the lawn is stressed out by other factors. And turf insects are even less of a problem than they once were, not because of any miracle bug-killer, but because of the grass itself. One of the major breakthroughs in recent plant breeding has been the development of insect-resistant grasses—new varieties that pests steer clear of.

These pest-resistant grasses are a result of making good use of a bad quality. Some pasture grasses, notably ryegrasses, have been perennially troublesome when they are infected with endophytes. These microscopic fungi don't hurt the plant—they exist in a symbiotic relationship—but cattle grazing on endophyte-infected grass become ill and may die.

However, around 1980 a little light went on over the heads of some turf breeders. If these tiny endophytes can harm a 1,000-pound steer, they reasoned, what might they do to a tiny weevil or chinch bug? In their research, these turf scientists learned that endophytes could kill those little pests. They also found out that many pests (evidently smarter than cows) would avoid grass infected with endophytes. And since we presumably don't have cows grazing on our lawns, the fungus would not present a hazard in turf grass.

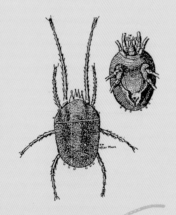

Because endophytes are passed from generation to generation through the seed, it was relatively easy to breed stocks of endophyte-infected, pest-resistant grasses. Today there are scores of these pest-proof grasses on the market. Among them are "Apache" tall fescue, "Repel," "Citation II," "Pennant," "Regal," "Prelude," and "All Star" perennial ryegrass.

That takes care of the most troublesome turf pests, except for one —the dreaded grub. These creepy little creatures, curled up in the soil, munching on plant roots, can do a lot of damage. If you see patches of brown grass that can be easily pulled up from the soil, you've got grubs. A few of them won't do a lot of damage. but five or more in a square-foot patch of turf exceeds the damage threshold.

Many of the pesticides once used to control grubs have been banned because they present environmental or human health hazards. Fortunately there are several kinder and gentler reme- dies. Merit, for example, is a synthetic pesticide manufactured by the Bayer Company that has proven effective against grubs at low application levels. Milky spore, a natural bacteria, can be applied to the soil to kill grubs. It's effective, but it works slowly, and results are poor in Northern regions where the soil temperature does not exceed 70 degrees for several months over the summer. Beneficial nematodes—microscopic soil-dwelling worms—have proven to be effective in hunting down and killing grubs underground.

THE SPIRITUAL LAWN OF NATURE

Living on asphalt and concrete, encased in steel and glass, answering to electronic summonses, we move farther and farther from nature. We catch a glimpse of parks through our windshields, and though we schedule time for the health club or masseuse or therapist, we rarely plan time to just be outdoors. But the lawn makes us schedule that time. The lawn is unrelenting in its demands. The lawn grows. The lawn must be mowed. For if it isn't, if we let it grow shaggy, then we violate the code of the lawn. So above all else, the lawn satisfies our powerful need to be in touch with nature. For many of us, the lawn may represent our only brush with the outdoors. We're isolated from nature until those summer weekends when we gravitate to the lawn to cook, to sit and nap, or to mow.

The lawn, at least, allows us some contact with the natural world, with plants that grow or languish and get sick and sometimes die. It allows, no, requires us to participate in the cycle of growth. Even if our hands never touch a blade of grass—and they rarely do—even if our own lawn-care calendar is out of touch with the growth cycle of the grass—and it often is—we're still in touch with the natural world.

Yet, ironically, we struggle to make that turf as unnatural as possible. We fight it to subvert its true nature and make it something that it isn't. We clip it to within an inch of its life. We pour on fertilizer. We douse it with pesticides. We drench it with water to keep it from going dormant. But no matter what its condition, the lawn allows us to fulfill the primal need to be in touch with the natural world.

---

the farm is still one of the prettiest in the state.

You might think that a sod farm would require intensive management and a heavy input of chemicals, that it would require vast amounts of fertilizer and especially herbicide to keep up the quality of the grass. And some do. But, amazingly, that's not the case here. Out of 300 acres in production, typically only 5 to 15 are treated with herbicide, and those only once per year.

"My father used to spray religiously," Roberts says, "but these fields have been in turf so long they really don't need it. The best prophylactic for weeds is a good stand of grass. The only reason we have weeds here is if the turf doesn't come up."

On his farm the turf is mainly tall fescue. To make a good stand, Roberts fertilizes, but not heavily. In fact, he believes that most homeowners fertilize too much. "Most homeowners are out of sync with what is good organic practice," he says. "The American male wants to fertilize between April 15 and May 15, when the weather's nice. But that is the worst time. If you fertilize then, you get a huge explosion of foliar growth. The grass gets soft and fluffy. And then the hot summer weather clobbers the grass."

Rather than feeding in the spring, Roberts recommends a fall fertilizing schedule. "The best time to fertilize in this part of the country is Thanksgiving weekend," Roberts says. "For moderate maintenance you should use a balanced fertilizer that supplies 1 pound of nitrogen per 1,000 square feet. If you want to fertilize twice, then fertilize in mid-October and again on Thanksgiving weekend."

7 GOING FOR THE GREEN

WE CAN RECOGNIZE the arrival of spring in the suburbs of America by the smell in the air. No, it's not the scent of blooming bulbs or cherry blossoms, but the acrid, nose-twitching odor of lawn fertilizer being spread by the ton from one end of town to the other. As soon as the snow melts or the weather warms just a bit, American men are on the move. We jump into our sport utility vehicles and head down to the garden center. There we load up with bags of lawn food with promising names like Turf Blaster, Super Green, and Lawn Miracle. Then we haul them home and pour the stuff on the lawn.

The lawn responds in a big way. Practically overnight it takes on an otherworldly greenish glow. All of that food does more than green up the grass; it also kicks it into overdrive. The grass shoots skyward. You can practically hear it growing from inside the house. So we mow. And mow again. The lawn mower barely has time to cool off before it's time to crank it up again. Grumble we may at all the work, but we also take some satisfaction in knowing that our act of kindness—fertilizing—has such a visible effect.

◄ For all the mowing and manicuring it receives, it's fertilizer that makes the golf course green.

We get almost instant feedback from feeding the grass. To us, that rich green color is like a grateful smile on the sated lawn.

But it doesn't last. So as soon as that smile fades, as soon as that green begins to lose its luster just a bit, we do it all over again—rush back to the store for another round of fertilizer.

In the midst of this binge and purge regime we rarely stop to wonder why we're force-feeding our turf—and making more work for ourselves. As men, and providers, it's our nature to offer support for those we love. And we do love our lawns. If we can do our duty without thinking, without agonizing, without getting to know the objects of our affection too well, hey, all the better. And if we can give them what we think they ought to need, even if it's not what they really require, we're happy.

And what could satisfy that urge better than fer-tilizing the lawn? Buy a bag of the stuff—it's cheap enough. Spend an hour or two spreading it with a lit-tle wheeled bin that's more of a toy than anything else we've had our hands on all week. We don't have to make an appointment or change our clothes. When we're done, our hands aren't even dirty. Within a few days, the lawn lets us know that we've done a good job, changing hue like a giant strip of litmus paper.

Yes, after the long, hard winter, we want to do something nice for our lawns. At the same time, we're impatient for them to shape up and snap out of the shabby spring doldrums. All winter long we've been watching golf on television. We've fallen asleep with visions of those glowing greens. (Why do you think they call them greens, anyway?) We want our lawns to look like those golf courses. They are the ultimate lawns, where grown men play a game for money—lots of money. The golf course is in the back of our minds when we stride onto the lawn. We imagine ourselves approaching the eigh-teenth green with the cameras rolling and the gallery erupting into applause.

We can, after all, identify with the golfers. They're not young, sculpted athletes. They look to be about our age. Maybe they have a little bit of a roll around the middle. And for uniforms they wear the same dorky polo shirts and chinos we buy at the mall and wear to barbecues. We are not so removed from them, and our lawns are not so removed from their playing fields. Not if we jack them up with fertilizer, they're not.

◄ Outside the clubhouse at the Robert Trent Jones Golf Club, a court-yard celebrates the sim-ple, irreplaceable unifying element of every course: healthy green grass.

Pounds of clippings generated annually by a 1,000-square-foot lawn: **200**

Pounds of nitrogen in 200 pounds of clip-pings: **8**

Pounds of nitrogen required annually by a 1,000-square-foot bluegrass lawn: **3**

Pounds of grass clip-pings disposed of in landfills in California alone annually: **6 billion**

SO YOU WANT TO BUILD A GREEN

Who hasn't dreamed of constructing a tournament-class putting green in the backyard? It can be done, if you're prepared to spend plenty of time and money and accrue significant frustration along the way.

➤ First, excavate a 1,000-square-foot area to a depth of 18 inches.

➤ Install 100 feet of drainage tiles and cover with a 4-inch-deep layer (approximately 12 cubic yards) of gravel.

➤ Cover the gravel with a 1½-inch-deep layer (4.6 cubic yards) of sand.

➤ Cover the sand with a 12-inch-deep layer (37 cubic yards) of topsoil.

➤ Level the surface and work soil into a fine seedbed.

➤ Sow creeping bentgrass in the North or hybrid Bermudagrass in the South.

➤ Purchase a greens mower (approximate cost: $5,000).

➤ Water daily.

➤ When grass sprouts and reaches ½ inch in height, mow to ¼ inch.

➤ Continue to water daily.

➤ Each morning, whisk the dew from the blades with a long pole.

➤ Mow daily to a height of ³⁄₁₆ inch to ⁵⁄₁₆ inch.

➤ During summer, water twice daily.

➤ Apply fungicides every ten days.

➤ Apply herbicides as needed.

➤ Aerate twice annually.

➤ Dethatch annually.

➤ Top-dress annually.

➤ Putt as time allows.

At Baltimore's Camden Yards, the grounds crew replaces a section of sod along the left field line. ➤ Ball park maintenance has not changed a great deal since the good old days at Yankee Stadium. By the end of the twentieth century, the artificial turf threat seems to have subsided; some fields are replacing their artificial turf with natural grass, and even retractable domed stadiums are now equipped with natural grass.

KEEPING THE FIELD GREEN

Pete Flynn may have the lawn-lover's dream job. Even after we give up our fantasies of pitching a no-hitter to clinch the pennant or driving in the winning run in the seventh game of the World Series, we can still dream of riding a mower across the infield of a major-league ballpark. That's what Pete Flynn does every single day of the baseball season. The head groundskeeper at Shea Stadium, he's been tending the field for the New York Mets for twenty-six years, ever since their inception.

It's not all fun and games for Pete, though. He has to worry about too much or too little rain, about diseases that would stick out like an error in the outfield, or weeds in the infield that could cause a ground ball to take a crazy hop. And then there are the players themselves, spitting sunflower seeds all over the field or refusing to use the on-deck circle and so wearing out the turf in front of the dugout. And then, he says with a hint of Irish brogue, "There's always the heat and humility."

Pete Flynn takes a lot of pride in his job. He knows that baseball just wouldn't be the same game of summer with-out that emerald-green field beneath the cleats of lanky outfielders loping after a fly ball in the sun. His lawn has to look good—all the time. You can't blame him if sometimes he feels a little unappreciated. "I don't think the fans understand what goes into maintaining a field," he says. "They think we have a lot of time to fix it when the team is on a road trip, but usually there's something else going on—a concert, a high-school or college game—even when the Mets are out of town."

In all, he's got about two acres of "Adelphi" Kentucky bluegrass to keep at its peak. With league expansion and extended playoffs, the season stretches from March to October, longer than the normal season for grass in Queens, so he has to work to get it to green up early and stay green all thorough the sea-son. To Pete that means you have to know and appreciate the grass. "Grass is like a woman," he says. "You've got to treat it nice to get the results you want."

Here's a look at how Pete Flynn treats the grass nice at Shea Stadium:

➤ Beginning in mid-March, fertilize every seven or eight weeks with about 100 pounds of 20-6-10, spread with a cyclone spreader at setting No. 5.

➤ Mow at ¾ of an inch height with a reel mower, daily on the infield, every second day on the outfield. To stripe the outfield, start at second base and mow directly toward the flag in center field. When you reach the warning track, turn and mow an adjoining strip back toward the infield. Repeat until the entire outfield has been mowed. It's the roller behind the blades of a reel mower that bends the blades of grass slightly and in an opposite direction with each pass to give the appearance of stripes.

➤ Treat with Dylene or other fungicide for leaf spot in rainy weather.

➤ Spot treat with an herbicide for weeds.

➤ Aerate twice a year with a machine that removes cores of soil and leaves them on top of the turf. Use a roller and hand rake to crush the cores and work them into the turf.

➤ Water as often as every day, as required.

➤ Resod worn patches of the field annually.

Is that something we should aspire to, though? Golf courses do not come by their perfect appearance naturally or easily. Most golf courses are totally artificial environments propped up by constant care. If that care stops, if they're neglected even for a few days, the system crashes. It takes dozens of men working full-time to keep a golf course looking good: laborers, greenskeepers, agronomists, toxicologists. They mow and water daily, fertilize every week, then apply herbicides, pesticides, and fungicides as often as every ten days to combat the weeds, insects, and disease that the high-maintenance program encourages.

However, some groundskeepers are beginning to question that high-input system and the effects of overfertilization, not only on the course but on the surrounding environment.

The Robert Trent Jones Golf Club in Lake Manassas, Virginia, is a showcase private club that's hosted some major tournaments, including the nationally televised Presidents Cup. You might assume that the groundskeeper there pours on the fertilizer (and pesticides) to keep it looking good. But you'd be wrong. In fact, the course has twice been awarded the Environmental Stewardship Award by the Golf Course Superintendents Association of America and was the first course in Virginia to be designated an Audubon Cooperative Sanctuary.

Construction began in 1988 on the course bordering a drinking-water reservoir, so those in charge

FERTILIZER PRESCRIPTION

Turf grasses have different appetites for fertilizer. Here are the nitrogen requirements for turf grass species in pounds of actual nitrogen per 1,000 square feet per year. "Actual nitrogen" refers to the total amount of nitrogen available in a fertilizer. It is indicated by the first of the three analysis numbers on the bag or box of fertilizer. Those numbers represent the percentage of actual fertilizer elements (nitrogen, phosphorus, and potassium, respectively) in the fertilizer. For example, a 100-pound bag of 10-6-4 will contain 10 pounds of actual nitrogen, 6 pounds of phosphorus, and 4 pounds of potassium. The rest of the mix will consist of fillers and perhaps small amounts of micronutrients.

Pounds of Actual Nitrogen per 1,000 Square Feet per Year

Species	Low Maintenance (FOR A BASIC GREEN LAWN)	High Maintenance (FOR A GREENER, FASTER-GROWING LAWN)
Bahiagrass	2	4
bentgrass	2	4
Bermudagrass	1	4
buffalograss	1	2
carpet grass	2	3
centipedegrass	2	4
fine fescue	1	2
Kentucky bluegrass	2	3
perennial ryegrass	2	3
St. Augustinegrass	2	4
tall fescue	1	2
zoysiagrass	2	3

of maintenance had to be especially aware of chemical runoff. The head groundskeeper, Glenn Smickley, embraced the challenge.

"When we built the course here, I knew the reservoir was an issue," Smickley says. "We wanted to make the community feel better about us." He felt he had a personal stake in the local environment, too. "Now, I'm not a tree-hugger," he says, "but I've got a wife and kids, and we bought a house nearby, and when all is said and done, we're drinking the

◄ The Robert Trent Jones Golf Club in Lake Manassas, Virginia, was built along a reservoir, so the groundskeepers have to consider the effects of fertilizer and pesticide runoff as they maintain the turf. Consequently, they've slashed their pesticide budget and cut synthetic fertilizer usage to virtually nothing.

diseases that the fertilizer encourages," he says. "So for the past four or five years, we haven't been fertilizing at all in the summer." He does virtually all of his fertilizing in the fall, when he applies about 1 pound of nitrogen per 1,000 square feet. That's far less than the 10 to 18 pounds per year recommended in some turf-management books, and even less than most homeowners use.

Smickley's secret is the soil. "If you take care of what's underneath," he says, "what's on top will take care of itself."

Soil, not just under a golf course, but any good soil, is populated by a civilization of microorganisms. Though there are generally a few bad actors—disease-causing fungi—most of them are good guys. And all of them can be sources of nutrients. One hundred pounds of

water, so I'm not going to pollute it."

Smickley has found, ironically, that maintaining the course environmentally hasn't been so difficult. On the contrary. "It's made my job easier," he says. "I don't have to be out there once a month with fertilizer or every week with a pesticide spray rig," he says. "And it's saved my budget, too." He's cut his annual pesticide budget from $80,000 to $30,000; where once he made ten to eleven fungicide applications annually to control pythium blight, now he has to apply those fungicides once every four to five years. He attributes the decreased disease pressure in large part to a drastic cut in fertilizer. "To me, excessive nitrogen in June, July, August, and September just means that more pesticides are needed to stop the

▲ ➤ In the old days, aerating was performed with contraptions such as this spring-loaded aerator or these spiked sandals. The vital process, which loosens compacted soil to allow better root growth and water penetration, is now mechanized.
➤ ➤ Glenn Smickley oversees the cultural practices at Robert Trent Jones, which has twice received the Environmental Stewardship Award from the Golf Course Superintendents Association of America.

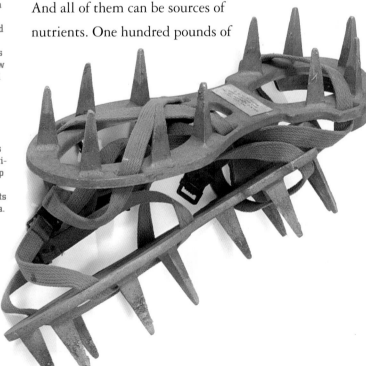

DECIPHERING THE BACK OF THE BAG

The sheer diversity of fertilizer formulas can make shopping for lawn food a bewildering experience. Generally, fertilizers with high analysis numbers give you more bang for the buck, but bigger isn't always better. The numbers on the front of the bag or box will give you a clue to the content, but check the small print on the back to determine whether the nitrogen is in a water-soluble or water-insoluble form. Water-soluble nitrogen dissolves quickly in the soil, so the nutrients are readily available. Because they are so soluble, however, they travel rapidly through the soil and are available for only a short time. If not absorbed by plant roots, they may leach into the groundwater. Most synthetic forms of nitrogen are water soluble.

Water-insoluble nitrogen, on the other hand, is not dissolved by soil moisture but must be released by the chemical action of micro-organisms in the soil. If you're impatient, that might not seem like a good thing, but if you're a grass plant, it is. Instead of a quick jolt of fertilizer, which shocks the plant, it provides a slow, gentle feeding. Most organic fertilizers contain water-insoluble nitrogen.

MILORGANITE

Just a bucket on wheels, with spinning arms to shoot fertilizer far and wide, the design of the rotary spreader hasn't changed in decades.

AMMONIUM SULFATE

ORGANIC BLEND

UREA

NITRATE OF SODA

A FERTILIZER MENU

Here are some of the common nitrogen sources you'll find in a bag of fertilizer.

ALFALFA MEAL
Percent actual nitrogen: 5
Availability: 2 weeks to 2 years
Comments: acidifying.

AMMONIUM NITRATE
Percent actual nitrogen: 34
Availability: immediate
Comments: acidifies soil; provides two forms of nitrogen.

AMMONIUM SULFATE
Percent actual nitrogen: 21
Availability: immediate
Comments: acidifies soil; good source of sulfur; used in evergreen food.

BAT GUANO
Percent actual nitrogen: 11
Availability: immediate to 2 months
Comments: acidifying; does not burn crops.

BLOOD MEAL
Percent actual nitrogen: 14
Availability: 2 weeks to 2 years
Comments: acidifying; quite expensive.

COTTONSEED MEAL
Percent actual nitrogen: 7
Availability: 2 weeks to 2 years
Comments: may contain pesticide residues.

COW MANURE
Percent actual nitrogen: 2
Availability: 2 weeks to 2 years
Comments: expensive in terms of dollars per pound of nitrogen.

FISH EMULSION
Percent actual nitrogen: 5
Availability: immediate
Comments: fastest-acting organic nitrogen source; contains trace elements.

FISH MEAL
Percent actual nitrogen: 5
Availability: immediate to 2 months
Comments: contains beneficial trace elements.

MILORGANITE
Percent actual nitrogen: 6
Availability: 2 weeks to 2 years
Comments: organic fertilizer from dried sewage sludge.

NITRATE OF SODA
Percent actual nitrogen: 16
Availability: immediate
Comments: neutral; fastest-acting natural product.

ORGANIC BLEND
Percent actual nitrogen: 5 to 10
Availability: 2 weeks to 2 years
Comments: usually contains a combination of dried manure, compost, and alfalfa meal.

POTASSIUM NITRATE
Percent actual nitrogen: 13
Availability: immediate
Comments: neutral; provides two nutrients but leaches easily; also high in potassium.

POULTRY MANURE
Percent actual nitrogen: 3
Availability: immediate to 2 months
Comments: acidifying; odiferous.

SULFUR-COATED UREA
Percent actual nitrogen: 38
Availability: days to weeks
Comments: alkalizing; released slowly over growing season; good for sandy soils.

UREA
Percent actual nitrogen: 46-0-0
Availability: 4+ days
Comments: alkalizing; may be toxic to seedlings.

UREAFORM
Percent actual nitrogen: 38
Availability: 4+ days
Comments: alkalizing; slower acting than urea; less easily volatilized.

◁ These days, it's not enough for the grass to be green at stadiums, ballparks, and golf courses. Superintendents sculpt the lawn, using a reel mower, to create visually striking patterns for the television audience.

microorganisms may contain up to 10 pounds of nitrogen, 5 of phosphorus, and 2 pounds of potassium. As they grow, consume, breed, and die, they release nutrients. Those microorganisms thrive in rich soils that are high in organic matter. "For every one percent organic matter you have in the top inch of soil, you can get up to a pound and a half of nitrogen released," says Smickley. So he renews the organic matter in his soil by using organic fertilizers. And he protects them by swearing off harsh, soil-damaging fertilizers. "We no longer use chlorine fertilizers," he says. "No potassium chloride. Though it's a cheap source of nutrients, the detriment from burning out your soil is far worse than any benefit."

In the past, when Smickley's turf started to look drab, his knee-jerk reaction was to hit it with a strong dose of nitrogen. "Now that's probably my ninth or tenth resort," he says. First he'll try to kick-start microbial reaction by applying a natural additive. "We'll spray humic acids to feed the microorganisms, then spray pure cane sugar or brewery extract to try to stimulate the feeding." He also applies fish emulsion at the recommended rate every ten days to provide trace amounts of nitrogen, plus micronutrients. But Smickley is not tied to a firm schedule. Instead, he lets the turf determine his care regime.

"Turf care is easier than most people believe," Smickley says. "Grass is a perennial plant. And guess what? It wants to stay alive. As long as it gets water, sunlight, and food, it's going to keep growing."

THE SPIRITUAL LAWN OF PRIVILEGE

How do we wear our manhood? We show our adult success and our power through our cars, our homes, our clothes . . . and our lawns. Even though our lawns are virtually identical—no, perhaps *because* they are all pretty much alike—we feel the need to differentiate them, to make our lawn the finest on the block. For the lawn is the welcome mat to our home . . . and our soul. It fills the eye when one approaches our house. It offers the first impression of us and how we live our life.

And from its beginning, the lawn has been an emblem of wealth and position. Two hundred years ago, only wealthy landowners could afford lawns. Early English lawns were patches of pasture dug up, planted, and kept cut by men with scythes. Because of the time and labor required to plant and tend these patches of turf, they took on additional significance. English lawns became symbols of success and prosperity.

Today the lawn still symbolizes prosperity. It's a sign that its owner possesses enough property that he can afford to devote his land to a crop that has no real material value.

It's true that the lawn has become democratized, but now, however, the owner's status is measured by the size and the condition of the lawn. (*Note: The American Association of Landscape Psychologists cautions that one should not base his or her own personal worth on the condition of plants in the landscape.*) A large, rolling swath of grass represents success. So does one that stays green all year, that's weed-free and as smooth as a pool table. The more pristine the lawn appears, the more refined it seems. Now that every man can have a lawn, the goal is to have the perfect lawn, and so we fertilize and water and spread chemicals, all to say to our neighbor, "I'm a success." On some level we all strive to have the biggest house, the newest car, the perfect family, and the best lawn.

So this lawn allows us to flaunt our success—to fuss and preen and show off.

◀ It's no coincidence that golf fairways resemble the savannas where the human race grew up. The rolling expanse of grass and scattered trees make us feel at home.

Smickley's light-handed care pays off. The Robert Trent Jones Golf Club has a much different feel from many courses. Maybe it's the absence of the chemical smell of fertilizers and pesticides in the air. Maybe it's the color of the grass underfoot—more natural, less Day-Glo. As you play the course, it doesn't take too much imagination to feel the soil churning with life under your feet. And perhaps, for a little while, you can feel the honest and pure spirit of the game of golf, the visceral attraction that pulled man to the course in the first place—the need to play a game. On this course it seems a little easier to shed the frustration and the competitiveness and remember that we play golf because it connects us with the earth. In contrast to our office-bound lives, walking the golf course makes the environment—grass, water, sand, trees, and air—a factor in our lives, something to be considered and worked with or around or against. It connects us, however tenuously, with our ancestors out on the savannas or prairies or plains on a quest, exerting our manhood in a place that feels like home.

DIET FOR A SMALL PLANT

LEAVE THE CLIPPINGS

If you routinely bag and dispose of grass clippings, you're throwing away a significant source of turf food. On a vigorously growing lawn, a year's worth of clippings from 1,000 square feet contains nearly 8 pounds of actual nitrogen. If left on the lawn—especially if they're chopped into small pieces with a mulching mower—the clippings will begin breaking down and releasing nitrogen within a matter of days.

FEED SPARINGLY

Most of us in the North get the lawn-feeding frenzy in early spring, but that's one of the worst times to feed a Northern lawn. Fertilize then and you're feeding cool-season weeds as well. And excessive fertilizer at this time of the year will force the grass into too much growth, setting it up for stress in summer. Instead, fertilize Northern lawns once in the fall, from September to November. The plants will store the food over the winter and be ready to get off to a fast start in spring. It's a different story in the South. There, turf needs early feeding to help it thrive through the summer heat. Southern grasses should be fertilized at least twice—in early summer and late summer—or as often as once a month, from May to August.

USE A KINDER, GENTLER FERTILIZER

Natural fertilizer sources usually contain water-insoluble nitrogen that is released slowly to provide a steady supply of food for the grass plant. They also encourage microorganisms.

TOP-DRESS

Top-dressing is a vital procedure for professional turf managers that remains a mystery to most homeowners. It's an easy way to improve the texture and fertility of your soil without digging up the lawn. Instead, spread a very thin layer of topsoil or organic matter such as sifted compost on top of the turf and let it work its way in. It's a surprisingly simple process:

➤ Use ¾ of a cubic yard of sifted compost or topsoil per 1,000 square feet.

➤ Apply in fall with a drop spreader in a layer no more than ⅜ inch thick.

➤ Water thoroughly.

WHITHER THE LAWN?

OUR FRONT LAWNS are under siege. It has become fashionable to trash the lawn. "It's a relic of a less enlightened time," the lawn-bashers say. They maintain that it's environmentally unsound—requiring high input of chemicals and precious water—and aesthetically trite. It seems that even that simple refuge of ours, the lawn, cannot escape the political correctness of our age. So we lawn aficionados are on the defensive, forced to hide our devotion to our beloved patch of green. Today, fussing over a lawn seems as shameful as smoking a cigarette or eating a double cheeseburger.

Where are the lawn-defenders? Where are the men who will stand up and say, "Mow we must"? Where are the men who will come to the aid of the lawn, who will ask not what the lawn can do for us but rather what we can do for our lawns? Men who will step forward to praise the lawn, not bury it under paving stones, ground covers, and weeds masquerading as wildflowers?

I say we need the lawn. All right, so maybe we don't need acres of it stretching to the horizon. Perhaps we don't need it to be putting-green short and totally weed-free.

◄ Maybe turf grass doesn't even need to be mowed, as the meadow and pasture creep into the neighborhood.

But we do need the lawn, not just for our psychological well-being, not only for its practical value, but because of its aesthetic virtues as well.

Even today's cutting-edge landscape architects and designers admit, sometimes grudgingly, that nothing can really replace a lawn.

"I don't know that people are as enamored with the lawn as in an earlier time," says Doug Reed of Douglas Reed Landscape Architecture in Cambridge, Massachusetts. "But it is true that the lawn is useful and practical. No matter how you cut it, turf grass is the most comfortable and functional material in the landscape." And he maintains that it serves a valuable function as a landscape element. "It's visually clean," he says, "and it appeals to the aesthetic of order and neatness."

The lawn is more problematic on the dry West Coast, where landscape architect Pamela Burton practices. Bright green irrigated lawns can look incongruous surrounded by the muted native vegetation. "In too many cases lawns look like someone has kicked over a can of green paint in the yard," Burton says. "Or they're treated like a piece of green cloth that you cut a pattern into rather than as one element of a contemporary design. But lawns can be wonderful design tools," she maintains. "They support the notion of creating space and help to determine the proportion of the whole landscape." In fact, when she takes on a job, she thinks that an existing lawn is a positive element, like the floor plan of a house. It provides some boundaries for her to work within.

Janice Hall, former apprentice to sculptor Isamu Noguchi and currently a partner in the landscape architecture firm of A. E. Bye and Janice Hall in New York City, says flatly, "I don't design lawns." In fact, she's loath to use the L-word. It has all kinds of negative connotations for her.

"The lawn that I grew up on was an American lawn in a classic sense," Hall says. "It was a perfect emerald green swath surrounding a colonial house. My father was very proud of it, and though I suppose my mother was also, it was really my father's terrain. When I think back to it," she says, "it was very

much like my mother's living room, where nobody ever went. Though she was very proud of it, it was not a room where we lived. The lawn outside was kind of like that. It never was alive; it was always the same. That was its appeal to my father: It was a constant that he could depend on."

Even though Hall maintains that lawn is a concept she doesn't relate to, her award-winning designs often contain expanses of grasses, either meant to be mowed or left alone as a high-grass meadow. "I think someone else might look at my work and say, 'Sure, there are lawns there,'" she admits.

So the lawn endures. But to survive, it must evolve. We can see the lawn with new eyes. Remake

◄ Concrete driveway pavers permit the turf to do double duty as a design element and as a parking area, much more interesting than asphalt or cement.
▲ Encroaching flower beds work to frame the lawn. In this case, less is more: The shrunken lawn is not only easier to care for, but it's also more visually attractive.

it and rehabilitate its image. To do that we can borrow the techniques of these landscape designers.

REDUCE IT

The first question landscape architects often ask is, "Do you really need all that grass?" And the answer is usually no. But we do need some for playing ball, for walking, for picnicking, and for just plain making our way around the rest of the landscape. Nothing beats turf grass as a surface for these pastimes, but other materials can replace it in the no-man's-land along the edges, where footsteps rarely fall.

"You can limit the lawn," says Pamela Burton. "You don't have to have lawn everywhere. So when we go in, we evaluate the property and determine how much turf is going to be necessary, and how it will be put to use."

Some clients insist on traditional lawns, she says. Others are amenable to turning the front yard over to more appropriate regional plantings. One, for example, opted for an olive grove and lavender garden in front of her house instead of grass. A small lawn was installed behind the house to provide a play area for her children.

There are many other alternatives. Doug Reed says, "When we have clients who find a large expanse of lawn boring, or too much to maintain, our solution depends on the overall design of the property. We may make dense areas of shrubs or trees out of open lawn or let portions go to meadow."

RESHAPE IT

Who says the lawn needs to be a rectangle? Zoning boards, developers, and contractors—that's who. The American lawn assumed its characteristic right-angled shape out of convenience, as it fit itself into suburban subdivisions. But it doesn't have to be that way. We can easily change the shape of the lawn by planting borders, beds, and shrub masses to make the lawn more fluid and visually interesting.

Janice Hall takes the reshaping of open grassy areas even further. When Hall starts a project with an existing expanse of lawn, she rethinks it, not just in terms of length and width, but in the third dimension of depth as well.

One of her recent projects demonstrates how powerful a lawn can be. The property, along the Massachusetts coast, was characterized "by a large and very bad lawn," she notes. "I knew it needed some work and decided immediately to sculpt the earth so that it would undulate like the water in the bay in the distance."

Patterns of light and shadow emerged as she walked the property, and she called in the bulldozers to help emphasize those existing patterns. One thousand cubic yards of soil later, the earth was transformed. "It wasn't just a surface thing anymore," she says. "Now it had volume and depth, flow and softness. As the feathery shadows slither across the earth, it becomes a participant in its surroundings." And grass, covering the earth, allows those patterns to

➤ The monochromatic two-dimensional lawn can serve as a canvas for sculptures and hardscape in the landscape.

show through. "Grass is ideal for that because it is so low to the ground and you can cut it any length that you want. With grass as a covering, the earth becomes very soft and nourishing; it really comes alive." No, Hall wouldn't call this grassy area a lawn. "But the owners do mow it," she admits. "And I've seen people go out and toss a ball around." Sounds like a lawn.

REVITALIZE IT

One of the defining qualities of a lawn is its immutability—always low, always green. But what if we (reluctantly) relinquish some of our control of the turf, leave it unmown or unwatered, and let the grass grow into what it wants to be? The results of letting the lawn's true texture and color show can be transforming, as seen on the grounds of the Thera-peutic Garden for Children in Wellesley, Massachu-setts, designed by Doug Reed. It demonstrates how grass can take on a whole new look when it's mowed at varying heights. At first Reed decided to allow the entire expanse of lawn to grow into a high-grass meadow. "It went to seed, and it was very beautiful," he says. But he admits that the effect was to make the property look abandoned. "So we mowed the ravines and paths so that it all felt managed, and it objecti-fied the meadow portion. Now it's even more beautiful and easier to maintain."

◄ ► How much grass does it take to make a lawn? That's the ques-tion landscape design-ers are asking, as they extricate the grass plant from the monoculture of the American lawn and integrate it into the landscape as a design element, bringing its own qualities—color, texture, and growth habits—to a patio or parking area.

Then Reed set his sights on the mown areas themselves. He bisected the lawn with a winding, 8-inch-wide steel rill with water flowing through. With sound and motion, the rill brings a vital new feeling to the lawn. Introducing other materials—steel and water—emphasizes his belief that the lawn is at its best where it serves as a counterpoint to hardscape materials or other vegetation. "A lawn can be an element that knits things together," he says, "an object within a garden; a field within which a number of other things are happening."

Pamela Burton, too, uses turf grass as counterpoint to other materials. In some of her most striking designs, she uses narrow strips of mown turf grass to frame large paving stones, or alternates strips of turf grass and concrete in a parking area. At

her own home she's planted a combination of buffalo-grass and blue grama grass to make green rectangles framed by native stone walls. The grass goes dormant in the heat of summer, but then it springs back and makes a soft and downy lawn.

Burton likes to let the true color of grass shine through, "unlike those steroid green Bermudagrass lawns or the turf that's painted green on the sod

farms," she says. "In normal years here we get as little as 7 to 8 inches of rain, so we try to think of the lawn as a piece of fabric that turns golden brown in the fall like the hills that mirror it."

REPLACE IT

Even the most adamant lawn-lovers must admit that in some parts of the country—notably the dry

Southwest—turf grass can be a high-maintenance item requiring regular irrigation, fertilization, and pest control to survive in an area to which it is not adapted. There, it may make sense to replace the turf grass with low-growing, spreading but drought-tolerant, and perhaps even native plants. There are plenty of candidates.

➤ OTHER GRASSES

Sheep fescue and blue fescue are somewhat less civilized cousins of the fine fescues. Though they do not make first-class conventional lawns, with their steely blue color, fine texture, and attractive mounding habit they make an attractive low-maintenance ground cover for out-of-the-way areas. buffalograss and blue grama grass, two American natives, can be mown to make a lawn, or they can be left unmown to serve as good ground covers.

➤ Here the lawn serves as a middle ground between the flat still blue of the pond and the raised and textured ornamental plantings in the border. It provides a vantage point from which to enjoy the surroundings, providing one with a quiet place to be. This lawn also happens to be indoors, in the conservatory at Longwood Gardens in Kennett Square, Pennsylvania.

◄ Gardeners are using alternative plants in difficult situations. Here, moss provides the look and feel of a lawn in the shade where turf grass struggles.

THE SPIRITUAL LAWN OF SAFETY

As we mow still deeper and deeper, the ancient power of the lawn takes hold over us. (Perhaps that's the reason for our desire for larger and larger lawns: The bigger they are, the longer it takes to mow, the more time there is for the lawn to work its spell over us.)

Out on the high-wire of our careers and lives, we yearn for safety. As we move from town to town, job to job, and advance from home to home, we're farther and farther from the touchstones that bring peace. We let go of our moorings. We've buried our parents. We've sold their goods. But we long for home.

And the lawn resonates with safety for reasons that we barely understand. The character of open space that defines a lawn accounts for the sensation of comfort that settles upon us as we stride across our suburban lots. It's a visceral response, says John Falk of the Smithsonian Institution, one that's locked deep in our DNA.

Falk has spent years studying not only the history of lawns but our relationship with them. Falk was struck by the similarity between the appearance of the classic suburban lawn and the savannas of Africa. He theorizes that our lawns appeal to a species memory of a home that we have never seen. The lawn, he suggests, is our best attempt to approximate the grassy expanse with scattered trees, the savannas where our species was born.

Throughout its history, turf has come to signify safety. Since prehistoric times, wild areas—jungles, forests, thickets of undergrowth—represented danger, where wild beasts, monsters, and witches could be lurking. *(Note: The Society for the Protection of Squirrels and Pigeons reminds us that these creatures do not represent a threat and should be warned when mowing will occur in their habitat.)* Clearing the land has always been the first order of business to keep dangers at bay. In tending our lawns, we may be responding to an instinct that compels us to clear our homestead, to remove wild growth that can harbor danger. Even though those primitive threats no longer exist, the primal need remains. The front lawn has become our demilitarized zone and a buffer against the wild.

So when we mow and fertilize and water, the lawn protects us, embraces and cradles us, and allows us, for a short time, to feel safe. Perhaps striding across a small stretch of land that resembles our "home" makes us feel safe and comfortable. For each of us, being on the lawn is like being back at our birthplace.

➤ **YARROW** This low-growing perennial stays green all summer, forming a thick, carpetlike covering 2 to 4 inches tall. It can also be mowed to 2 inches to remove the flowers. Drought-tolerant and cold-hardy, yarrow grows well in full sun in well-drained soil.

➤ **SEDGES** Many of the members of the *Carex* genus are North American natives that resemble our common turf grasses. With their low growth and spreading or creeping habits, they make a fine grass substitute. When species are grown in their native areas, they require very little maintenance. Some good choices are catlin sedge for the Southwest, cedar sedge for Texas and the Gulf states, and Pennsylvania sedge for the East.

➤ **CHAMOMILE** This small flowering plant has been used for centuries to make elegant and sweetly scented lawns. However, it requires full sun and very well drained soil and does not withstand traffic well. In some situations, a chamomile lawn may require more maintenance than turf.

➤ **OTHER GROUND COVERS** Ivies, *Pachysandra,* lily of the valley, and other creeping or spreading perennials make good grass substitutes for the shade.

➤ Meadow gardens get more sophisticated. Instead of just tossing wildflower seeds to the wind, gardeners fine-tune mixtures to create elegant meadows such as this one with white daisies, blue cornflowers, and red clover.

THE FUTURE OF THE LAWN

Twenty years ago our vision of the future of the lawn included Astroturf carpets spread across the suburbs, robotic mowers that would tend the lawn on their own while we reclined in a hammock, growth hormones that would eliminate mowing by stunting the growth of grass, and pesticides that would free the lawn of weeds, insects, and diseases forever. Today, predictions for the American lawn look quite a bit different.

➤ The lawn will shrink, no doubt about it, and be replaced by meadows, prairies, woodlands, and hardscaping.

➤ What there is of the lawn will consist of a new breed of grasses that require much less maintenance: perhaps only two mowings a year, little fertilizer, no pesticides.

➤ Designers will continue to experiment with turf grass as a design element, planting a combination of turf grass species in strips and geometric patterns and using turf grass to create paths through more wild plantings.

➤ Heavily trafficked areas of turf grass will be replaced by hardscaping that can be lived on, like paving stones or inert ground covers such as decomposed granite.

SOURCES

WEB SITES

FLORIDA TURF CYBERLINKS

http://floridaturf.com/cyberturf.htm

University of Florida site contains links to turf associations, golf sites, and botany pages.

GREENNET

http://www.greenindustry.com

Turf and landscaping industry site with on-line publications, calendar of events, and product links.

GROUNDS MAINTENANCE MAGAZINE

http://www.grounds-mag.com/calendar.htm

Publication for landscape professionals includes a complete calendar of turf trade shows and seminars.

PROFESSIONAL LAWN CARE ASSOCIATION OF AMERICA

http://www.plcaa.org

Association of turf managers and landscapers offers news releases, calendar of events, and links to other turf sites.

TEXAS A&M TURFGRASS LINKS

http://soilcrop.tamu.edu/turf/links/links.html

Links to universities, turf societies, and commercial turf companies plus a grass identification program.

ASSOCIATIONS

THE LAWN INSTITUTE

1509 Johnson Ferry Rd. NE
Suite 190
Marietta, GA 30062
404-977-5492
http://www.lawninstitute.com/

Provides lawn fact sheets and variety recommendations for the industry and for homeowners.

TURF PRODUCERS INTERNATIONAL

1855-A Hicks Rd.
Rolling Meadows, IL 60008
847-705-9898
http://www.turfgrassSod.org

Formerly the American Sod Producers Association. Provides complete information on sod.

U.S. LAWN MOWER RACING ASSOCIATION

1812 Glenview Rd.
Glenview, IL 60025
847-729-7363
E-mail: letsmow@aol.com
http://www.letsmow.com/uslmra

For complete information on USLMRA rules and membership and schedule of races.

PLACES TO VISIT

THE BRITISH LAWNMOWER MUSEUM

106-114 Shakespeare St.

Southport, Kancashire, England

(44) 170-453-5369

Fax: (44) 170-450-0564

http://www.dspace.dial.pipex.com/town/square/gf86/

Displays include lawn mowers of the rich and famous and racing lawn mowers. Open year-round.

THE INTERNATIONAL LAWN, GARDEN, AND POWER EQUIPMENT EXPO

Kentucky Exposition Center

Louisville, KY

502-562-1962

An annual event featuring the largest collection of lawn mowers and lawn tools in the country, with 500,000 square feet of indoor displays and 17 acres outdoors.

THE LAWN AT THE UNIVERSITY OF VIRGINIA

University of Virginia

Charlottesville, VA 22903

As the centerpiece of "Thomas Jefferson's Academical Village," this stretch of turf was one of the first public lawns in the United States.

THE MUSEUM OF GARDEN HISTORY

Lambeth Palace Rd.

London, England

(44) 171-401-8865

Garden artifacts, including lawn equipment, housed in an old cathedral.

REEL LAWN MOWER HISTORY & PRESERVATION PROJECT AT NORTH FARMS

30 North Farms Rd.

Haydenville, MA 01039-9724

http://www.crocker.com/~jricci/

Society to preserve hand, horse, and motor mowers, with a collection of more than 100 machines.

THE RESORT AT SQUAW CREEK

400 Squaw Creek Rd.

P.O. Box 3333

Olympic Valley, CA 96146

800-327-3353

A pesticide-free golf course.

TRERICE MANOR

Kestel Mill

Newquay, Cornwall, England

(44) 163-787-5404

Site of the famous Halford collection of old lawn mowers. Open to the public from April to October.

U.S. GOLF ASSOCIATION MUSEUM AND LIBRARY

P.O. Box 708

Liberty Corner Rd.

Far Hills, NJ 07931

908-234-2300

Home of the United States Golf Association; houses a library, research center, golf artifacts, and a ball-hitting robot.

UNIVERSITIES

Many university turf departments hold annual field days to display new varieties and techniques at their turf trial grounds. Check with your state university for a schedule or contact one of the following.

CLEMSON UNIVERSITY
Clemson, SC 29631
803-656-3311

OREGON STATE UNIVERSITY
Corvallis, OR 97331
503-737-0123

THE PENNSYLVANIA STATE UNIVERSITY
University Park, PA 16802
814-865-4700

RUTGERS
THE STATE UNIVERSITY OF NEW JERSEY
New Brunswick, NJ 08903
908-932-1766

TEXAS A&M UNIVERSITY
College Station, TX 77843
409-845-8484

UNIVERSITY OF FLORIDA
Gainesville, FL 32611
352-392-7939

UNIVERSITY OF NEBRASKA
Lincoln, NE 68583
402-472-7211

GRASS SEED

AGRITURF
59 Dwight St.
Hatfield, MA 01038
413-247-5689
Specializes in ecologically sound turf seed mixes.

BLIGHT NATIVE SEEDS
Jim and Kevin Blight
Box 244
Oakville, Manitoba
Canada, R0H 0Y0
204-267-2376
Fax: 204-267-2699
Specializes in native and low-maintenance grasses.

CORNHILL MARKETING LIMITED
Dept. YG806
10 Lowes Lane Industrial Estate
Wellesbourne
Warwick, England CV35 9RB
(44) 178-947-0055
Purveyors of grass seed.

GARDENS ALIVE!
5100 Schenley Pl.
Lawrenceburg, IN 47025
812-537-8650
Lawn seed mixes, organic lawn fertilizers, and pest control products.

JACKLIN SEED COMPANY

West 5300 Riverbend Ave.

Post Falls, ID 83854

208-773-7581

Breeders and retailers of improved turf seed.

JONATHAN GREEN

P.O. Box 326

Farmington, NJ 07727

800-526-2303

General seed catalog, offering many lawn mixes and blends.

LAWNORDER

P.O. Box 8219

Essex, VT 05454

800-522-2193

http://www.lawnorder.com/

Complete supply of hard-to-find turf seed for shade, drought, and insect resistance. Also a full line of weeding and other lawn-care tools, and organic fertilizers and pesticides.

LEVINGTON HORTICULTURE

Paper Mill Lane

Bramford, Ipswich

Suffolk, England IP8 4BZ

(44) 147-383-0492

Fax: (44) 147-383-0386

(44) 147-383-0046

Distributor of turf food.

LOFT'S SEED INC.

Bound Brook, NJ 08805

800-526-3890

http://www.turf.com/

Breeders and retailers of some of the most advanced turf seed on the market.

NICHOLS GARDEN NURSERY

1190 North Pacific Hwy.

Albany, OR 97321

503-928-9280

Good source for Ecolawn mix containing wildflowers and turf.

O. M. SCOTT'S & SONS COMPANY

14111 Scottslawn Rd.

Marysville, OH 43041

513-644-4277

Complete line of seed mixes and fertilizers.

PENNINGTON SEED

P.O. Box 290

Madison, GA 30650

800-282-SEED

800-285-7333

http://www.penningtonseed.com/

Choice turf seed for the South.

PLANTS OF THE SOUTHWEST

Agua Fria

Rt. 6 Box 11A

Santa Fe, NM 87505

800-788-SEED

Specializes in native, low-maintenance plants, including grasses.

LAWN MOWERS

ALLEN POWER EQUIPMENT LIMITED

The Broadway
Didcot, Oxon
England OX118ES
(44) 123-551-5400
E-mail: Sales@allenpower.com
Manufactures the Lawncycler Hover Mower, which rides on a cushion of air, and other turf tools.

AMERICAN LAWN MOWER/ GREAT STATES CORPORATION

22 E. Washington St. #400
Indianapolis, IN 46204
317-631-0260
The country's largest manufacturer of push reel lawn mowers.

HUSQVARNA FOREST & GARDEN LTD (HVA)

Oldends Lane, Stonehouse
Gloucestershire, England GL 10 3SY
(44) 145-382-2382
Fax: (44) 145-382-6936
http://www.international.husqvarna.com/
Manufactures the AutoMower, a battery-powered robotic lawn mower, as well as conventional riding mowers and hand tools.

JOHN DEERE & COMPANY

4401 Bland Rd.
Suite 200
Raleigh, NC 27609
919-954-6420
http://www.deere.com/
Specializes in riding mowers and lawn tractors.

RYOBI AMERICA COMPANY

5201 Pearman Dairy Rd.
Suite 1
Anderson, SC 29625
800-525-2579
Manufacturers of battery-powered lawn mowers.

SIMPLICITY MANUFACTURING COMPANY

500 North Spring St.
Port Washington, WI 53074
414-284-8669
http://www.simplicitymfg.com/
Manufactures riding mowers.

SNAPPER

P.O. Box 777
McDonough, GA 30253
770-957-9141
Manufacturer of professional-quality riding mowers and garden tractors for the home.

SUNLAWN IMPORTS

326 Garfield St.
Fort Collins, CO 80524
970-493-5284
Fax: 970-493-5202
E-mail: sunlawn@webaccess.net
http://www.sunlawn.com/
Imports a precision push reel mower from Germany.

THE TORO COMPANY

8111 Lyndale Ave. South

Minneapolis, MN 55420

612-888-8801

http://www.toro.com/

One of the oldest power mower manufacturers in the United States.

WOLF GARDEN MANUFACTURING

Crown Business Park

Tredevar

Gwent, England NP24EF

(44) 149-530-6600

Manufactures The Cart, a light, sporty riding mower that resembles a go-cart.

TOOLS, FERTILIZERS, AND OTHER LAWN SUPPLIES

A. M. LEONARD

241 Fox Dr.

Piqua, OH 45356

800-543-8955

http://www.amleo.com/

Venerable tool company. For many years a source of all manner of horticultural tools for professionals and amateur gardeners alike. Good source of hand-weeding tools for the lawn.

AMES LAWN & GARDEN TOOLS

P.O. Box 1485

Mansfield, OH 44901

http://www.ames.com/

Complete source for spades, shears, and weeding tools.

GARDENERS SUPPLY COMPANY

128 Intervale Rd.

Burlington, VT 05401

800-863-1700

Good source for organic lawn-care products, as well as hand tools.

HARMONY FARM SUPPLY

3244 Hwy. 116 N A

Sebastopol, CA 95472

707-823-9125

Fax: 707-823-1734

E-mail: info@harmonyfarm.com

Tools, books, sprinklers, and organic fertilizers.

LAWN-EDGIT

Box 82543, 300 Taunton Rd. E

Oshawa, Ontario, L1G 7W7

905-404-2992

Fax: 905-404-2992

E-mail: lawn-edgit@sympatico.ca

Lawn edging material.

MILORGANITE

1101 North Market St.

Milwaukee, WI 53202

414-225-3225

Organic fertilizer manufactured from sewage sludge.

PEACEFUL VALLEY FARM SUPPLY

P.O. Box 2209
Grass Valley, CA 95945
530-272-4769
Fax: 530-272-4794
E-mail: contact@groworganic.com
http://www.groworganic.com/
Complete selection of organic fertilizers as well as tools.

RUGG MANUFACTURING

105 Newton St.
Greenfield, MA 01301
800-633-8772
http://www.rugg.com/
Distributors of the Back Savr Easy Weeder, a lawn weeding tool.

SCOTTS MIRACLE-GRO PRODUCTS INC.

800 Port Washington Blvd.
Port Washington, NY 11050
800-645-8166
E-mail: consumer.services@scottsco.com
http://www.miracle-gro.com/
Liquid lawn fertilizer and hose end sprayers.

SEA-BORN/LANE INC.

1601 13th Ave.
Charles City, IA 50616
800-457-5013
Fax: 515-228-4417
E-mail: jdunkel@fia.net
http://www.home.fia.net/~jdunkel/seaborn.htm
Natural lawn fertilizers, including seaweed, kelp, bone, blood, fish meals, rock phosphate, greensand, diatomaceous earth.

SMITH & HAWKEN

35 Corte Madera Ave.
Mill Valley, CA 94941
800-776-3336
http://www.smith-hawken.com/
Push reel mowers and many hand tools.

SNOW & NEALLEY

P.O. Box 876
Bangor, ME 04402
http://www.sntools.com/
Catalog of quality hand tools, including the fish-tail dandelion weeder.

TRUGRIND

32 Brolans Gardens
Hornchurch
Essex, England RM112AE
(44) 017-084-4348
Manufacturer of lawn mower sharpening tools.

TURK SCYTHES & TRIMFLEX

18 Spiers Way
Horley
Surrey, England RH6 7NY
(44) 129-378-5069
Distributor of turf hand tools.

WALT NICKE COMPANY

P.O. Box 433
Topsfield, MA 01983
508-887-3388
Unusual and useful hand tools.

BIBLIOGRAPHY

Building a Healthy Lawn: A Safe and Natural Approach by Stuart Franklin, 1988, Storey Books.

Chemical-Free Lawn: The Newest Varieties and Techniques to Grow Lush, Hardy Grass, The by Warren Schultz, 1989, Rodale Press.

Driving the Green: The Making of a Golf Course by John Strawn, 1991, Lyons & Burford.

Grass Varieties in the United States by James Alderson and W. Curtis Sharp, 1995, Lewis Publishers.

Handbook of Successful Ecological Lawn Care by Paul D. Sachs, 1996, Edaphic Press.

Healthy Lawn Handbook, The by Lane L. Winward, 1992, The Lyons Press.

Home Lawn Handbook, The (Plants and Gardens, Vol. 29, No. 1) by Henry Indyk, 1988, Brooklyn Botanic Garden, Inc.

How to Get Your Lawn and Garden Off Drugs: Pesticide Free Gardening for a Healthier Environment by Carole Rubin, 1989, Friends of the Earth.

IPM Handbook for Golf Courses edited by Gail L. Schumann et al., 1997, Ann Arbor Press, Inc.

Lawn: A History of an American Obsession, The by Virginia Scott Jenkins, 1994, Smithsonian Institution Press.

Lawn Care for Dummies by Lance Walheim and the National Gardening Association, 1997, IDG Books Worldwide.

Natural Insect Control by Janet Marinelli and Warren Schultz, 1994, Brooklyn Botanic Garden Inc.

Natural Lawn & Alternatives, The by Janet Marinelli and Margaret Roach, 1993, Brooklyn Botanic Garden Inc.

New Lawn Expert, The by D. G. Hessayon, 1997, pbi Publications.

Redesigning the American Lawn: A Search for Environmental Harmony by F. Herbert Bormann, 1995, Yale University Press.

Safe & Easy Lawn Care: The Complete Guide to Organic, Low-Maintenance Lawns (Taylor's Weekend Gardening Guides) by Barbara Ellis, 1997, Houghton Mifflin.

Smart Yard: 60-Minute Lawn Care by Jeff Ball and Liz Ball, 1995, Fulcrum Publishing.

Turfgrass Management by A. J. Turgeon, 1995, Prentice Hall.

Turfgrasses: Their Management and Use in the Southern Zone by Richard L. Duble, 1996, Texas A&M University Press.

Wild Lawn Handbook: Alternatives to the Traditional Front Lawn, The by Stevie Daniels, 1995, Macmillan.

INDEX

*All of the photographs in this book are by Roger Foley except for
the following:*

Corbis-Bettman: pages 10, 41, 76, 96

Culver Pictures, Inc.: pages 12, 17, 30, 32, 34, 40, 100

Rosemary Schultz: page 13

Courtesy of the Library of Congress: pages 14, 25, 28, 29, 31 (left),
    79, 139

Christie's Images: pages 20, 21, 22

Smithsonian Institution, Archives of American Gardens: pages 23, 35,
    37, 78

Smithsonian Institution, National Museum of American History:
    pages 33, 101

William Schlelsner (courtesy of the Library of Congress): page 41

Cynthia Woodyard: pages 48, 49

Douglas Reed: pages 60, 150, 152, 153

Dency Kane: pages 74, 75, 162, 165

Barbara Woike: page 95

Courtesy of Novartis Crop Protection: pages 114–20, 149

Allan Mandell: pages 154–61